T0270620

Disrupting the Chinese Military in Competition and Low-Intensity Conflict

An Analysis of People's Liberation Army Missions, Tasks, and Potential Vulnerabilities

TIMOTHY R. HEATH, ERIC ROBINSON, CHRISTIAN CURRIDEN, DEREK GROSSMAN, SALE LILLY, DANIEL EGEL. GABRIELLE TARINI

Prepared for the United States Army
Approved for public release; distribution is unlimited

For more information on this publication, visit **www.rand.org/t/RRA1794-2**.

About RAND

The RAND Corporation is a research organization that develops solutions to public policy challenges to help make communities throughout the world safer and more secure, healthier and more prosperous. RAND is nonprofit, nonpartisan, and committed to the public interest. To learn more about RAND, visit www.rand.org.

Research Integrity

Our mission to help improve policy and decisionmaking through research and analysis is enabled through our core values of quality and objectivity and our unwavering commitment to the highest level of integrity and ethical behavior. To help ensure our research and analysis are rigorous, objective, and nonpartisan, we subject our research publications to a robust and exacting quality-assurance process; avoid both the appearance and reality of financial and other conflicts of interest through staff training, project screening, and a policy of mandatory disclosure; and pursue transparency in our research engagements through our commitment to the open publication of our research findings and recommendations, disclosure of the source of funding of published research, and policies to ensure intellectual independence. For more information, visit www.rand.org/about/research-integrity.

RAND's publications do not necessarily reflect the opinions of its research clients and sponsors.

Published by the RAND Corporation, Santa Monica, Calif.
© 2023 RAND Corporation
RAND® is a registered trademark.

Library of Congress Cataloging-in-Publication Data is available for this publication.

ISBN: 978-1-9774-1157-0

Cover: Xinhua / Alamy Stock Photo.

Limited Print and Electronic Distribution Rights

About This Report

This report documents research and analysis conducted as part of a project entitled *Army Special Operations Roles and Priorities in Competition with China*, sponsored by the United States Army Special Operations Command (USASOC). The purpose of the project was to identify and prioritize potential contributions of Army special operations forces to efforts to impose costs, create dilemmas, and affect adversarial decisionmaking to advance U.S. influence and erode adversary influence during competition and in key contingencies involving China.

This research was conducted within RAND Arroyo Center's Strategy, Doctrine, and Resources Program. RAND Arroyo Center, part of the RAND Corporation, is a federally funded research and development center (FFRDC) sponsored by the United States Army.

RAND operates under a "Federal-Wide Assurance" (FWA00003425) and complies with the *Code of Federal Regulations for the Protection of Human Subjects Under United States Law* (45 CFR 46), also known as "the Common Rule," as well as with the implementation guidance set forth in DoD Instruction 3216.02. As applicable, this compliance includes reviews and approvals by RAND's Institutional Review Board (the Human Subjects Protection Committee) and by the U.S. Army. The views of sources utilized in this report are solely their own and do not represent the official policy or position of DoD or the U.S. government.

Acknowledgments

We are indebted to the many representatives of the U.S. special operations community who supported this effort, and we are particularly thankful for insights from the soldiers and civilians at USASOC Headquarters, 1st Special Forces Command, 4th Psychological Operations Group, 8th Psychological Operations Group, 95th Civil Affairs Brigade, U.S. Special Operations Command Pacific, and the Office of the Assistant Secretary of Defense for Special Operations and Low-Intensity Conflict. We are especially thankful for support from our sponsors within USASOC Headquarters, including COL Joseph Wortham, Matthew Carran, Larry Deel, Mike Malli, Brooke Tannehill, and Damon Cussen.

We also thank the leadership of the RAND Arroyo Center for its support throughout this project, including Sally Sleeper, Molly Dunigan, Jonathan Wong, Stephen Watts, and Jennifer Kavanagh (now of the Carnegie Endowment for International Peace). We also thank our reviewers, Joel Wuthnow of the National Defense University and Kristen Gunness of RAND.

Summary

For the first time since contending with the Soviet Union in the Cold War, the United States faces the prospect of a long-term strategic competition with a near-peer rival: the People's Republic of China.[1] The U.S. 2022 National Defense Strategy declares that China represents "the most comprehensive and serious challenge to U.S. national security" in its attempts to "refashion the Indo-Pacific region and the international system to suit its interests and authoritarian preferences."[2] Although the risk of war remains low, the possibility that tensions might escalate to the point of conflict cannot be discounted.

In this report, we expand on a comprehensive list of potential People's Liberation Army (PLA) missions that has been developed in prior research;[3] builds a detailed list of PLA tasks required to execute key competition and low-intensity conflict missions; and, more importantly, identifies potential vulnerabilities in the ability of the PLA to execute these tasks in pursuit of Beijing's strategic objectives. Our goal with this research was to inform planning efforts by the United States to constrain the Chinese military's ability to harm U.S. interests. Our analysis involved a review of publicly available documents regarding China's foreign policy goals and PLA missions, tasks, and capabilities as explored in prior research. From these materials, we developed plausible Chinese peacetime military tasks to support the country's efforts to outcompete the United States and considered potential vulnerabilities in their execution.

We also drew from an academic literature review regarding great-power war to explore analogous PLA tasks and vulnerabilities in a hypothetical U.S.-China low-intensity conflict. Low-intensity conflict could also include a variety of hybrid or irregular warfare methods, such as cyberattacks, information warfare, and gray-zone activities involving paramilitary forces. China uses some of these methods today, of course. The difference in a scenario of low-intensity conflict would be a more extensive use of such tactics that would overlap with a greater willingness to carry out violent actions against the United States. These possibilities are not mutually exclusive—China could use many of these methods simultaneously. Geographically, the conflict could occur across much of the world, just as the peacetime U.S.-China competition has already become globalized. In particular, the expansion of Chinese

---

[1] White House, *National Security Strategy of the United States of America*, December 18, 2017.

[2] U.S. Department of Defense, *2022 National Defense Strategy of the United States of America*, October 27, 2022, p. 4.

[3] Specifically, we leverage the Chinese Communist Party Defense Strategy Mission Framework developed in Timothy R. Heath, Derek Grossman, and Asha Clark, *China's Quest for Global Primacy: An Analysis of Chinese International and Defense Strategies to Outcompete the United States*, RAND Corporation, RR-A447-1, 2021, p. 64; and the low-intensity conflict defensive and offensive missions developed in Timothy R. Heath, Kristen Gunness, and Tristan Finazzo, *The Return of Great Power War: Scenarios of Systemic Conflict Between the United States and China*, RAND Corporation, RR-A830-1, 2022, p. 83.

interests in countries in Eurasia, Africa, the Middle East, and Latin America increases the possibility that, in the event of conflict, China might use military force to defend its interests in many locations. A U.S.-China low-intensity war could feature a broad variety of confrontations that occur sequentially or simultaneously across the world.

Our analysis focuses on 16 total offensive and defensive missions as they have been defined in prior research, split evenly between peacetime competition and low-intensity conflict.[4] Across these various missions, we develop 31 separate tasks that are implicit in the PLA's efforts to execute each mission in accordance with Beijing's strategic guidance. We derive and assess specific roles for PLA forces in these tasks; likely operational approaches; and potential coordination between the PLA and nonmilitary Chinese actors across the diplomatic, intelligence, and propaganda components of the Chinese government. Most importantly, we identify a variety of vulnerabilities that could affect the ability of the PLA to successfully execute each task.

Stressing these vulnerabilities could disrupt Beijing's ability to achieve its national objectives, although doing so could, in some cases, also yield adverse effects for the United States. We emphasize that these vulnerabilities are hypotheses that will require further investigation and research to validate. However, the following five broad types of vulnerabilities emerge from our analysis:

- **Fears of Chinese domestic instability:** These vulnerabilities arise from the potential for actions taken by the PLA to exacerbate internal tensions in China. The vulnerabilities could arise from excessive repression, politicization of the military, or domestic blowback from casualties or embarrassing military failures.
- **Escalation risk:** These vulnerabilities arise from the potential for actions taken by the PLA to drastically worsen and destabilize a situation, resulting in unwanted expansion of conflict, protraction, or damage to China's economic prospects.
- **Reputational risk:** These vulnerabilities arise from the potential for actions or a lack of action taken by the PLA to result in severe costs to China's reputation, influence, and appeal as a partner.
- **Limited ability to support partners:** These vulnerabilities arise from limitations on the PLA's ability to operate with partners and motivate them to fight on China's behalf.
- **Limited ability to project power:** These vulnerabilities arise from constraints on the PLA's ability to conduct military operations far from the Chinese mainland.

These vulnerabilities should not be seen as potential silver bullets that, if exploited, could lead to immediate mission failure by the PLA; they are vulnerabilities that, if targeted, could disrupt China's ability to achieve higher-order strategic goals, such as shaping a favorable international environment or ensuring sustained economic growth. Moreover, targeting these vulnerabilities could, in some cases, result in unwanted escalation or other undesirable

---

[4] Heath, Grossman, and Clark, 2021, p. 64; Heath, Gunness, and Finazzo, 2022, p. 83.

outcomes. The vulnerabilities represent a framework for understanding potential constraints on Chinese strategic design and decisionmaking in the ability to achieve national strategic objectives through military power in situations short of high-end war. Further research is required to weigh the potential merits and drawbacks of potential U.S. actions against the vulnerabilities.

Implications for the United States

This report explores the implications that these vulnerabilities have for potential future efforts by the United States to disrupt China's ability to leverage the PLA to achieve its national strategic objectives. In this report, we apply a framework and logic for strategic disruption by U.S. military forces in competition that has been developed in a companion report.[5] This framework is used to generate initial implications regarding opportunities to disrupt Chinese strategic objectives in competition and low-intensity war. We explore three ways that the United States could leverage the PLA's vulnerabilities to frustrate Beijing's preferred strategies of using the PLA to achieve core objectives:

- The United States could deter harmful PLA actions by shaping perceptions of the potential negative effects of those actions to China's own interests.
- The United States could exploit the adverse consequences of PLA actions after they occur to deter Beijing from repeating similar actions.
- The United States could exploit specific PLA weaknesses in power projection and partner support to weaken Beijing's confidence in the PLA and discourage similar operations and activities.

From these mechanisms, we summarize a set of broader opportunities for potential strategic disruption campaigns that exploit the PLA's primary vulnerabilities in peacetime competition and low-intensity conflict:

- To target reputation-related vulnerabilities, the United States could illuminate and amplify evidence of PLA coercion and overreach. These revelations could impair China's ability to build partnerships abroad and could more actively deter harmful Chinese actions. If U.S.-China tensions escalated to the point of war, damage to China's reputation could harm its efforts to build coalitions against the United States.
- To target vulnerabilities related to escalation, the United States could increase pressure on Chinese client states to mire PLA forces in an unwanted conflict, particularly in the course of a low-intensity conflict.

---

[5] Eric Robinson, Timothy R. Heath, Gabrielle Tarini, Daniel Egel, Mace Moesner, Christian Curriden, Derek Grossman, and Sale Lilly, *Strategic Disruption by Special Operations Forces: A Concept for Proactive Campaigning Short of Traditional War*, Santa Monica: RAND Corporation, RR-A1794-1, 2023.

- To target vulnerabilities in China's ability to support partners, the United States could highlight and amplify evidence of the PLA's limited ability to assist partners with their security needs.
- To target vulnerabilities in the PLA's ability to project power, the United States could highlight the military's limited ability to protect Chinese citizens and interests abroad.

Contents

Figures and Tables

Figures

Tables

CHAPTER 1

Introduction

For the first time since contending with the Soviet Union in the Cold War, the United States faces the prospect of a long-term competition with a near-peer great power: the People's Republic of China.[1] The U.S. 2022 National Defense Strategy declares that China represents "the most comprehensive and serious challenge to U.S. national security" in its attempts to "refashion the Indo-Pacific region and the international system to suit its interests and authoritarian preferences."[2] The size of China's economy is second only to that of the United States, although it continues to lag in per capita income by a wide margin. The People's Liberation Army (PLA) has rapidly modernized to the point that it can now hold at risk the success of any U.S. military intervention along China's periphery.

This narrowing of the gap in national strength between the United States and China has coincided with a deepening of broader disputes over trade, technology transfer, cyber espionage, human rights, and other issues.[3] U.S.-China relations remain strained over long-standing flash point issues, such as Taiwan and the South China Sea. Moreover, Chinese leaders have stepped up their criticism of U.S. international leadership and called for China to take a larger role in global leadership instead. Chinese leaders have demanded that the United States abandon its alliances in the Asia-Pacific, for example, even as they outline a vision for a reconstructed security architecture premised on Chinese power, norms, and ideals.[4] Chinese authorities frankly acknowledge the inevitability of competition with the United States, although they reject the idea that war is inevitable.[5] Indeed, despite a heightening of U.S.-China tensions, most observers regard the prospect of war as extremely low. Nevertheless, given the severity of the rivalry, the possibility that tensions might escalate to the point of conflict at some point in the future cannot be fully discounted.[6]

---

[1] White House, *National Security Strategy of the United States of America*, December 18, 2017.

[2] U.S. Department of Defense, *2022 National Defense Strategy of the United States of America*, October 27, 2022, p. 4.

[3] Franco Ordoñez, "U.S., China Accuse Each Other of Mishandling COVID-19," NPR, March 23, 2020.

[4] State Council Information Office, *China's Policies on Asia-Pacific Security Cooperation*, January 2017.

[5] "Commentary: China, U.S. Can 'Cooperate' to Make Bigger Pie for Lunch," Xinhua, May 6, 2019.

[6] James Dobbins, Andrew Scobell, Edmund J. Burke, David C. Gompert, Derek Grossman, Eric Heginbotham, and Howard J. Shatz, *Conflict with China Revisited: Prospects, Consequences, and Strategies for Deter-*

In this report, we analyze potential vulnerabilities in the Chinese military's execution of missions and tasks to achieve strategic goals both in peacetime competition with the United States and in a hypothetical scenario of low-intensity, indirect war between the United States and China. This report expands on a comprehensive list of potential People's Liberation Army (PLA) missions developed in prior research,[7] builds a list of PLA tasks required to execute key competition and low-intensity conflict missions, and explores associated vulnerabilities in the ability of the PLA to execute these tasks. The goal of this research is to inform planning efforts by the United States to constrain China's ability to leverage its military instrument of power to harm U.S. interests short of a large-scale high intensity war.

In a previous report, RAND researchers examined the U.S.-China competition from a whole-of-government perspective.[8] China has generally relied on its economic strength and diplomatic outreach to achieve its foreign policy objectives; the PLA has played, at most, a supporting role. This dynamic is true for its current strategy to outcompete the United States as well. In a typical formulation, Chinese Foreign Minister Wang Yi stated that "competition is normal," but he warned that "exaggerating competition will squeeze the space for cooperation."[9] China's view is informed by its assessment of the relative decline of the West and rise of the non-West. It is also informed by long-standing Chinese grievances against U.S. international leadership. Since at least the mid-2010s, Chinese officials have increasingly characterized U.S. international leadership as incompatible with China's needs. In 2016, for example, senior diplomat Fu Ying compared the existing U.S.-led international order and its compatibility with China to "an old suit that no longer fits."[10]

Although we recognize the primacy of economics and diplomacy in China's approach to strategic competition, we focus on the role of the military in this report for several reasons. First, our study was designed to support U.S. military planning. Thus, focusing on the military dimension of the competition is most immediately relevant to our purposes. Second, we assess that the PLA will play a larger role in China's foreign policy in coming years. China's military is already capable of carrying out a variety of nonkinetic operations to both defend Chinese interests and hinder U.S. influence abroad. These peacetime tasks consist of nonwar operations, actions, and activities designed to generally strengthen China's strategic position and weaken the positions of the United States and its allies. Investments in the PLA's power

---

rence, RAND Corporation, PE-248-A, 2017.

[7] Timothy R. Heath, Derek Grossman, and Asha Clark, *China's Quest for Global Primacy: An Analysis of Chinese International and Defense Strategies to Outcompete the United States*, RAND Corporation, RR-A447-1, 2021, p. 64; Timothy R. Heath, Kristen Gunness, and Tristan Finazzo, *The Return of Great Power War: Scenarios of Systemic Conflict Between the United States and China*, RAND Corporation, RR-A830-1, 2022, p. 83.

[8] Heath, Grossman, and Clark, 2021.

[9] "China, U.S. Stand to Gain from Cooperation, Lose from Confrontation: Foreign Minister," Xinhua, March 8, 2019.

[10] Fu Ying, "The US World Order Is a Suit That No Longer Fits," *Financial Times*, January 6, 2016.

projection capabilities—which include long-range transport, marines, and cyber and space capabilities—and continued improvements in the PLA's experience operating abroad should strengthen its ability to contribute to foreign policy tasks. Officials have also noted an uptick in the PLA's military diplomacy. For example, China's 2019 defense white paper declared that "a new configuration of foreign military relations which is all-dimensional, wide-ranging and multi-tiered is taking shape," citing increasing military exchanges between the PLA and "more than 150 countries."[11]

Beyond the PLA's role in peacetime competition, we consider the possibility that the competition could escalate to conflict. In this report, we explore potential PLA missions and tasks that could be relevant in the event of a long-duration conflict with the United States. However, we deliberately chose not to focus our analysis on the possibility of a major high-intensity war between the United States and China, partly because considerable research has already explored how a major war might unfold near Taiwan.[12] More importantly, some analysts have pointed to hybrid war and other variants of low-intensity war as a more likely form of U.S.-China conflict because of the dangers of escalation in high-end war.[13]

To be clear, there is no publicly available information to suggest that China is contemplating a global, low-intensity war with the United States. However, a lack of Chinese attention does not negate the possibility that such low-intensity wars could occur. Irregular or low-intensity conflicts have historically been unanticipated by mainstream military thinkers at the time, many of whom subsequently struggled to understand their dynamics. For a handful of examples, Napoleon's forces were surprised by the ruthless guerrilla war in Spain, U.S. military planners largely failed to anticipate the protracted trajectory of the Vietnam War, and Soviet planners failed to adequately prepare for an unconventional war in Afghanistan. Similarly, U.S. and Chinese military thinkers might focus on preparing for conventional combat operations, but unexpected developments could drive both sides to an indirect form of conflict for which they might not have planned. To date, very little research has explored this potential in detail. We hope to contribute to this important topic with this report.

Potential Forms of U.S.-China Low-Intensity Conflict

A low-intensity conflict between the United States and China could take many forms, as the United States and Soviet Union learned in their struggle against one another in the Cold

---

[11] State Council Information Office, *China's National Defense in the New Era*, July 24, 2019, p. 31.

[12] See, for example, David C. Gompert, Astrid Stuth Cevallos, Cristina L. Garafola, *War with China: Thinking Through the Unthinkable*, RAND Corporation, RR-1140-A, 2016, and Jan van Tol, Mark Gunzinger, Andrew F. Krepinevich, and Jim Thomas, *Air Sea Battle: A Point of Departure Concept*, Center for Strategic and Budgetary Assessments, 2010.

[13] Shira Efron, Kurt Klein, and Raphael S. Cohen, *Environment, Geography, and the Future of Warfare: The Changing Global Environment and its Implications for the U.S. Air Force*, RAND Corporation, RR-2849-5-AF, 2020.

War. As in the Cold War, the United States could find itself supporting a partner government against China-backed nonstate actors, perhaps in the Americas or the Middle East. In such distant regions, the PLA's limited power projection capability would make large-scale Chinese military intervention unlikely, but arms sales and support to nonstate actors could aim to exhaust U.S. military resources in a protracted conflict. The reverse is also possible. Low-intensity conflict could take the form of U.S. support for nonstate actors that are engaged in hostilities against a Chinese-backed government. In yet other cases, both sides might back either rival states or nonstate groups in another country. Low-intensity conflict could also include a variety of hybrid or irregular warfare methods, including cyberattacks, information warfare, and gray-zone activities that involve paramilitary forces. China already uses some of these methods. In a scenario of low-intensity conflict, the difference would be a more extensive use of such tactics and a greater willingness to carry out violent acts in pursuit of war aims against the United States. These possibilities are mutually exclusive; some or all types of confrontation could occur simultaneously.

Geographically, the conflict could occur across the world just as the peacetime U.S.-China competition has already become globalized. In particular, the expansion of Chinese interests in countries in Eurasia, Africa, the Middle East, and Latin America increases the possibility that China might use military force to defend its interests in the same countries in the event of instability. A U.S.-China low-intensity conflict could feature a broad variety of conflict situations that occur sequentially or simultaneously around the world. Our analysis does not presume a specific time frame for such a conflict, but, for the purpose of structuring our analysis, we posit that conflict would not erupt until at least after the year 2030. We emphasize that this is merely a planning assumption, not a prediction.

War, even of a low-intensity nature, very likely would affect every aspect of life in the United States and China. Each government could be expected to deploy whole-of-government resources in the pursuit of victory. In such a war, the United States could be directed to target both military and nonmilitary aspects of China's broader war effort. Although the nonmilitary dimensions of such a conflict are important, a comprehensive review of all potential Chinese whole-of-government actions and activities in a low-intensity conflict with the United States lies beyond the scope of this report. We focus instead on the military dimension of China's approach to competition and a hypothetical low-intensity conflict with the United States. Even if our analysis is confined to the military dimension alone, the variety of potential lines of analysis is enormous. The preparation and fielding of Chinese military forces, research and development of new weaponry, and political warfare are just some of the potential topics that could be covered. We have chosen to focus on the missions and tasks of Chinese military and paramilitary forces that might engage U.S. forces and partners both to bound our analysis and because these missions and tasks would likely pose the most-immediate threats. We aim to directly support planning by describing the types of vulnerabilities in PLA missions and tasks that the United States could counter to protect its interests.

Methodology

Our analysis focuses on 16 total offensive and defensive missions as defined in prior research and split evenly between peacetime competition and low-intensity conflict.[14] Across these various missions, we develop 31 separate tasks that are implicit in the PLA's efforts to execute each mission in accordance with Beijing's strategic guidance. We derive and assess specific roles for PLA forces in these tasks; likely operational approaches; and potential coordination between the PLA and nonmilitary Chinese actors across diplomatic, intelligence, and propaganda components of the Chinese government. Most importantly, we identify a variety of vulnerabilities that could affect the ability of the PLA to successfully execute each task.

To produce this analysis, we examined unclassified Chinese and non-Chinese official documents, news reports, and scholarly writings. We collected and summarized current knowledge about Chinese intentions for the nation's goals, especially regarding foreign policy and defense topics. High-level official documents that outline the national priorities of the ruling Chinese Communist Party, such as President Xi Jinping's report to the 19th Party Congress,[15] and authoritative statements of Chinese foreign and defense policies, such as government white papers and speeches by top leaders (including Xi) were especially valuable. Analysis of articles by Chinese scholars and experts in such journals as *Seeking Truth* [求实], *People's Daily* [人民日报], *Outlook* [瞭望], *Modern International Relations* [现代国际关系], *Chinese Military Science* [中国军事科学], and *PLA Daily* [解放军报] complement authoritative sources with insight into the meaning and logic of key concepts and directives.

Using this source material, we explore plausible national strategic and military goals for how Chinese authorities might seek to outcompete the United States and reach their goals of national revival.[16] In constructing these strategies, we have tried to adhere as closely as possible to the frameworks, logic, and goals of Chinese authoritative sources. We readily acknowledge that the strategies, missions, and tasks proposed in this study unavoidably involve some degree of informed speculation to fill in gaps not explicitly addressed in Chinese documents. In summary, although we have tried to provide a plausible road map for Chinese strategic competition with the United States, we emphasize that this is ultimately an analytic construct worthy of continued refinement.

Regarding the potential for low-intensity conflict, we emphasize that we aim to provide a structured analytic framework designed to stimulate creative thinking about future possibilities for war and support defense planning that is focused on disrupting potential Chinese vulnerabilities in such a scenario. Therefore, this scenario is not a prediction. It is an exercise in structured, scenario-based analysis. Yet, to be valuable, our analysis should be as rigorous and data-informed as possible. We acknowledge that Chinese officials have not publicly

---

[14] Heath, Grossman, and Clark, 2021, p. 64; Heath, Gunness, and Finazzo, 2022, p. 83.

[15] "Full Text of Xi Jinping's Report at 19th CPC National Congress," Xinhua, November 3, 2017.

[16] This analysis builds on similar discussion in Heath, Grossman, and Clark, 2021, and Heath, Gunness, and Finazzo, 2022.

discussed, nor do they seem to desire or anticipate, a potential low-intensity conflict with the United States. Chinese scholarly sources are similarly silent on this possibility. Although Chinese military thinkers have generally focused on conventional war, they have shown increased interest in hybrid and irregular war beginning around the 2010s. Chinese analysts have studied Russian hybrid wars as an example and particularly note the use of information operations and proxies.[17] Zhang Jiadong, a professor at the Center for American Studies at Fudan University, theorized a type of conflict that he labeled *multiborder war*, one fought by actors including politicians, technicians, and business professionals through almost any means necessary. Such a war, he notes, would "blur the boundary between peace and war."[18] Similarly, Wang Xiangsui, an irregular warfare expert of the PLA Air Force (PLAAF), published a book in 2021 in which he discusses the concept of hybrid warfare as a form of conflict in "which material destruction is never the purpose."[19]

In our analysis, we draw from well-established sources about the roles and missions of China's military forces in peacetime to explore how they might change in conflict. We consider available military and paramilitary forces that China has in its inventory that could be employed in an irregular or hybrid confrontation with the United States. We also incorporate insights from previous RAND reports on how great-power wars start and persist.[20] From this base of knowledge, we derive a set of missions and tasks that Chinese military forces might execute.

Although we sketch out a variety of assumptions to frame our analysis, the main point of analyzing a potential low-intensity conflict between the United States and China is not to predict its outcome or narrate how it might unfold but to describe the types of vulnerabilities that PLA forces might face in their execution of operations during a low-intensity war.

---

[17] Duan Junze [段君泽], "Russian 'Hybrid Warfare' Application and Its Influence," [俄式 "混合战争" 实践及其影响], *Modern International Relations* [现代国际关系], 2017, p. 3. Unless otherwise indicated, the authors of this report provided the translations of bibliographic details for the non-English sources included in this report. The original rendering in Chinese appears in brackets after the English translation.

[18] Zhang Jiadong [张家栋], "Multi-Border War: The Possible Form of Future War" [多边疆战争：未来战争的可能形态], *Frontiers* [人民论坛·学术前沿], 2021.

[19] Wang Xiangsui [王湘穗], "Analysis of Future Hybrid Warfare" [未来混合战争形式解析], *Military Digest* [军事文摘], 2021, p. 13.

[20] See, for example, Dobbins et al., 2017; Gompert, Stuth Cevallos, and Garafola, 2016; Heath, Gunness, and Finazzo, 2022; Jacob L. Heim and Benjamin M. Miller, *Measuring Power, Power Cycles, and the Risk of Great-Power War in the 21st Century*, RAND Corporation, RR-2989, 2020; and Michael J. Mazarr, Samuel Charap, Abigail Casey, Irina A. Chindea, Christian Curriden, Alyssa Demus, Bryan Frederick, Arthur Chan, John P. Godges, Eugeniu Han, Timothy R. Heath, Logan Ma, Elina Treyger, Teddy Ulin, and Ali Wyne, *Stabilizing Great-Power Rivalries*, RAND Corporation, RR-A456-1, 2021.

Chinese Military Forces and Regional Groupings

China has a variety of armed forces with which it could execute security-related missions and tasks in both peacetime and wartime. Not only does Beijing command the uniformed PLA, it has available such paramilitary services as the People's Armed Police (PAP), Chinese Coast Guard (CCG) and the maritime militia. We refer to many of these groups in discussing potential PLA tasks. For context, in the following section, we briefly survey the military and nonmilitary actors that are most likely to be involved in relevant missions and tasks. We also consider the global scale of China's competition in peacetime and the possibility that a low-intensity systemic war with the United States could spread to other parts of the world as well. To facilitate this analysis, we provide geographic groupings, which are derived from categories developed in official Chinese foreign policy writings and discussed further in the "Regions" section, in which relevant PLA missions are likely to occur.

Chinese Armed Forces and Nonmilitary Actors

China has both military and nonmilitary resources to execute missions and tasks for competition and low-intensity war (Table 1.1). Within the military, there are five services: the PLA Ground Force (PLAGF), PLA Navy (PLAN), PLAAF, PLA Rocket Force (PLARF), and PLA Strategic Support Force (PLASSF). The PLAGF consists of ground combat forces and is responsible for land warfare. The PLAN and PLAAF are composed of traditional naval and air force units, respectively. The PLARF employs the nation's land-based ballistic and cruise-missile capabilities, including nuclear weapon systems. In 2016, Beijing established the PLASSF to carry out cyber, electronic warfare, psychological, and space operations.[21]

Although these are the principal military services, other specialized units relevant to this analysis consist of the PAP, PLA Navy Marine Corps (PLANMC), PLA Joint Logistics Support Force (PLAJLSF), PLA Special Operations Forces (PLA SOF), CCG, and People's Armed Forces Maritime Militia (PAFMM). The PAP is a paramilitary unit that augments law enforcement forces with internal security duties. It also is responsible for counterterrorism activities. The PLANMC carries out some missions abroad and is responsible for amphibious assault operations against small islands. The PLAJLSF is responsible for providing logistics support to joint operational forces, such as those that might be deployed abroad in a hypothetical low-intensity conflict. PLA SOF are the special operations units of the PLA responsible for special reconnaissance and elite light infantry assignments. There are PLA SOF units in the PLAGF, PLAN, PLAAF, and PAP. Ostensibly, the CCG is a maritime constabulary force, but in reality it is fully integrated with the military's command and control.[22] Similarly,

---

[21] Kevin L. Pollpeter, Michael S. Chase, and Eric Heginbotham, *The Creation of the PLA Strategic Support Force and Its Implications for Chinese Military Space Operations*, RAND Corporation, RR-2058-AF, 2017.

[22] Yew Lun Tian, "China Authorises Coast Guard to Fire on Foreign Vessels If Needed," Reuters, January 22, 2021.

TABLE 1.1

Responsibilities of Chinese Military and Nonmilitary Services and Bureaucracies

Service, Unit, or Organization	Responsibilities
PLAGF	Land warfare
PLAN	Naval warfare
PLAAF	Air warfare
PLAJLSF	Logistics support to the joint forces
PLARF	Land-based ballistic and cruise missile capabilities, including nuclear weapons
PLASSF	Cyber, electronic warfare, psychological, and space operations
PLA SOF	Special operations warfare
CAC	Chief censorship body
UFWD	CCP organization responsible for recruiting nonparty organizations and individuals to promote CCP interests
International Liaison Department	CCP agency responsible for establishing and maintaining relations with foreign political parties
Propaganda-media	Chinese state media and propaganda entities, including Xinhua News Agency, People's Daily, PLA Daily, State Council Information Office, and the Propaganda Ministry.
MFA	Government ministry responsible for foreign policy
State Council	Top administrative government body that reports directly to the CCP top leadership
TAO	Government office handling all Taiwan-related policy
Provincial Governments	Subnational governments that at times support national level policy requirements
PSC	Private entities owned by Chinese state-owned enterprises (SOEs), supporting local security abroad

SOURCES: Features information from Office of the Secretary of Defense, *Military and Security Developments Regarding the People's Republic of China 2021*, U.S. Department of Defense, November 3, 2021; U.S. Central Intelligence Agency, *The World Factbook*, 2022.

NOTE: CAC =Cyberspace Administration of China; UFWD = United Front Work Department; MFA = Ministry of Foreign Affairs; TAO = Taiwan Affairs Office; PSC = private security companies.

the PAFMM poses as a fleet of civilian fishing boats but in fact receives training and arms from the PLAN and is fully integrated with the military's command network.[23]

Finally, there are several nonmilitary Chinese organizations that would likely support many of the PLA's missions or operate alongside it in pursuit of their own tasks. China's vari-

---

[23] Gregory B. Poling, Harrison Prétat, and Tabitha Grace Mallory, *Pulling Back the Curtain on China's Maritime Militia*, Center for Strategic and International Studies, November 18, 2021.

ous ministries are notoriously stovepiped. Therefore, coordination between the military and nonmilitary offices remains a challenge in peacetime and likely would remain so in conflict as well. The National Security Commission, established in 2013, would play a critical coordinating role in all activities. Other relevant ministries and organizations outside the PLA would include the CAC, the UFWD, the MFA, propaganda-media organizations, the State Council Information Office, TAO, provincial governments, and PSCs.

The CAC is the chief regulating body of the Chinese internet. The CAC has the ability to censor unfavorable and propagate favorable Chinese Communist Party (CCP) narratives to the Chinese populace. The UFWD is a department in the CCP that is responsible for building coalitions of supporters in non-CCP entities both in China and around the world. The CCP's International Liaison Department is responsible for establishing and maintaining relations with foreign political parties. China's MFA is the primary implementer of Chinese diplomacy.

China's government also relies on a broad array of state-owned propaganda and media outlets. Because it is an authoritarian regime, the line between media and propaganda is often blurred. In this report, we use the shorthand *propaganda-media* to refer to these entities, which include Xinhua, the official news agency of the state; the *People's Daily*, the newspaper of the CCP Central Committee; the Propaganda Ministry, the government bureaucracy responsible for censoring content and directing official messaging; and the State Council Information Office, which is the government's primary office for external propaganda and messaging. The State Council is the top administrative body and reports directly to the CCP on all matters of policy. The TAO handles all policy related to Taiwan. Provincial governments sit below the national-level governmental structure and at times can play a role in implementing national policy matters.

PSCs are commercial entities that have security-related duties. China has 5,000 PSCs, about 20 to 40 of which operate abroad.[24] Chinese PSCs are generally owned by the state enterprises; often staffed by PLA veterans; and primarily focused on intelligence collection, training of host nation forces, and escort duties. They do not engage in combat operations and generally do not carry firearms. However, a small number of PSCs are authorized to carry firearms, specifically those involved with sea marshal duties. In the future, China could rely on PSCs to augment PLA units operating abroad, most likely along Belt and Road Initiative (BRI) routes.[25] The BRI aims to integrate the Eurasian landmass through China-led infrastructure and trade efforts.[26]

---

[24] Max Markusen, "A Stealth Industry: The Quiet Expansion of Chinese Private Security Companies," Center for Strategic and International Studies, January 12, 2022.

[25] Jingdong Yuan, "China's Private Security Contractors and the Protection of Chinese Economic Interests Abroad," *Small Wars and Insurgencies*, Vol. 33, No. 1–2, 2022.

[26] Jennifer Hillman and Alex Tippett, "Who Built That? Labor and the Belt and Road Initiative," Who Built That? Labor and the Belt and Road Initiative," *The Internationalist*, blog, Council for Foreign Relations, July 6, 2021.

Regions

How the PLA executes missions in either peacetime competition or low-intensity conflict is likely to vary by geographic region. Missions that might be appropriate in some regions might not be in others because of the potential for escalation, the strength of China's relationship with relevant actors, or the importance China places on a particular region.

To facilitate the development of our list of PLA missions and tasks, we identified several distinct geographic regions for future PLA military operations (Figure 1.1), and we refer to these regions throughout the report. These regions are our categorizations, not China's, but they are loosely based on comparable geographic groupings that Chinese foreign policy specialists have described. Most major foreign policy documents and directives adhere to a tiered grouping of countries, generally categorized as (1) major developed countries, such as the United States, countries in the European Union, and China; (2) countries along China's periphery, i.e., the Indo-Pacific; (3) developing countries, which include the nations of the global south; and (4) multilateral organizations, including the United Nations and regional multilateral groups (such as the Shanghai Cooperation Organization). China's government has adhered to this pattern to provide a predictable, recognizable template to guide its own instructions to foreign policy workers. This pattern can be seen in the foreign policy section of the 19th Party Congress report and the recent foreign policy white paper, for example.[27]

For purposes of our study, we simplify the Chinese designations into four categories: (1) China (including disputed territories in the first island chain); (2) the Indo-Pacific; (3) Europe, Africa, the Middle East, and the Americas; and (4) the United States. We omit multilateral organizations because, although they are important for China's foreign policy, they are less relevant in the context of specific military competition and conflict missions.

Report Organization

This report is structured in the following manner. In Chapter 2, we describe the military's role in China's peacetime strategy to outcompete the United States. We describe Beijing's potential success criteria for competition and the set of missions that the military might be assigned to support that strategy. We describe the variation in tasks that the Chinese military might engage in by geographic region. The PLA faces challenges in executing many of these tasks, and we analyze potential vulnerabilities for each of them.

In Chapter 3, we explore a scenario of systemic, low-intensity war between the United States and China. The prospect of such a conflict remains low. Thus, dramatic changes in the U.S.-China relationship would necessarily precede the onset of such a conflict. Drawing from previous academic research, we briefly summarize the most-plausible changes that might appear during a transition from current strategic competition to low-intensity war

---

[27] "China's International Development Cooperation in the New Era," Xinhua, January 10, 2021; "Full Text of Xi Jinping's Report at 19th CPC National Congress," 2017.

FIGURE 1.1

Assessed Geographic Regions for Chinese Military Operations

Region 1: China
Region 2: Indo-Pacific
Region 3: Europe, Africa, Middle East, and Americas
Region 4: United States

and identify a handful of other general assumptions to frame our analysis. We then present a set of likely missions for the PLA in a low-intensity conflict, which would be modified from those required for peacetime competition, and break each mission down into discrete tasks that PLA forces could conduct during a systemic, low-intensity conflict that spans much of the globe. As with our analysis of peacetime competition, we analyze potential vulnerabilities that the PLA might face in conducting its missions.

In Chapter 4, we summarize our findings and explores their implications for efforts by the United States to exploit these vulnerabilities as a way of disrupting China's ability to leverage force to achieve its national strategic objectives. We apply a framework and logic for strategic disruption by U.S. military forces in competition, which has been developed in a companion report, to generate initial implications and avenues for future analysis of opportunities to disrupt Chinese strategic objectives in competition and low-intensity war.[28] We conclude with some recommendations and an appendix that summarizes the various PLA missions, tasks, and vulnerabilities as analyzed in this report in Chapter 5.

---

[28] Eric Robinson, Timothy R. Heath, Gabrielle Tarini, Daniel Egel, Mace Moesner, Christian Curriden, Derek Grossman, and Sale Lilly, *Strategic Disruption by Special Operations Forces: A Concept for Proactive Campaigning Short of Traditional War*, RAND Corporation, RR-A1794-1, 2023.

CHAPTER 2

China's Peacetime Competition Strategy

In this chapter, we analyze a comprehensive list of PLA missions and tasks that most directly support Chinese efforts to outcompete the United States. We begin with a brief discussion of Beijing's desired end state for U.S.-China relations, and its strategy to achieve that end state. We then introduce a set of likely PLA missions in peacetime competition as drawn from prior research. For each mission, we then develop a comprehensive set of potential tasks for the PLA to execute to achieve Beijing's underlying strategic goal for each mission, and we identify and analyze potential vulnerabilities in the PLA's ability to achieve those objectives.

Chinese authorities frankly acknowledge the reality of competition with the United States but reject the notion that conflict is inevitable.[1] This perspective suggests that Beijing recognizes the importance of managing competition with the United States in a manner that avoids war. No official Chinese document that outlines a strategy for managing competition with the United States is known to exist. If it does exist, its contents have not been made available to the public, nor should we expect that it would because of the sensitivity of the topic. However, the Chinese government has provided numerous documents on its broader foreign policy objectives. Relevant sources include Party Congress reports, speeches by President Xi Jinping, and government foreign policy and defense white papers. Moreover, Chinese scholars and analysts associated with central government institutes and academies have published extensively on the topic of U.S.-China relations. These documents, many published by scholars associated with the central government, help illuminate the meaning and intent of official directives. From this material, we deduce a Chinese strategy to outcompete the United States that is largely consistent with China's observed behavior.

China has generally relied on its economic strength and diplomatic outreach for much of its foreign policy; the PLA has played, at most, a supporting role. This dynamic is true for its current strategy to outcompete the United States as well. Although we recognize the primacy of economics and diplomacy in great-power competition, we focus our analysis on the role of China's military forces specifically.

In the following sections, we explore the key missions and tasks that the PLA has or is likely to have as a part of China's peacetime competition strategy. For each task, we list the relevant PLA and non-PLA forces that are likely to be involved and relevant geographic regions.

---

[1] "Commentary: China, U.S. Can 'Cooperate' to Make Bigger Pie for Lunch," 2019.

We also explore potential vulnerabilities that Chinese military forces could face in executing these tasks. These vulnerabilities provide a sense of the difficulties that the PLA could face in accomplishing its objectives. They also underscore the challenges that CCP decisionmakers could face in using military power to achieve foreign policy objectives. We reiterate that these vulnerabilities represent analytic hypotheses and are worthy of further research and validation. However, they are analytically informed baseline assessments that are intended to promote further thinking on ways to disrupt and counter Chinese peacetime strategies that might threaten U.S. interests.

Beijing's Desired National End State: The China Dream

The starting point for analyzing China's strategy to outcompete the United States is to understand Beijing's overriding strategic goals for the nation's development. China's leadership has declared an intention to realize the country's revitalization as a great power by midcentury, an end state that authorities under Xi Jinping have hailed as the *China Dream*. This vision of national rejuvenation involves comprehensively increasing the standard of living for Chinese citizens and overseeing the country's revitalization as a wealthy, premier world power under CCP leadership by the centenary of the founding of the People's Republic of China in 2049.[2]

China's Assessed End State for U.S.-China Relations[3]

Any strategy for competition with the United States is likely to be nested under the overarching pursuit of the China Dream. China's end state implies a downgrading in the position of the United States to accommodate China's ascent to the center of the international economy and geopolitics. Beijing could accordingly and reasonably expect the United States to resist its supersession. Hinting at this concern, Chinese commentary routinely hurls accusations that the United States seeks to maintain its "hegemonic position" by containing China's rise.[4] The U.S. government has consistently rejected the accusation that it seeks to "contain" China. However, U.S. authorities have criticized China's refusal to adhere to the "rules-based order," which Beijing claims is inherently biased to support U.S. interests.[5]

A strategy to outcompete the United States would therefore need to deal with potential U.S. resistance while setting the conditions for China's successful ascent. The point of any

---

[2] "Full Text of Xi Jinping's Report at 19th CPC National Congress," 2017.

[3] For a broader assessment of China's strategy and desired end-state for U.S.-China relations, see Heath, Grossman, and Clark, 2019. This section expands on the analysis provided in that report.

[4] Liu Xin, "U.S. Escalates Containment of China by Targeting China's Influence on UN: Analyst," *Global Times*, June 17, 2021.

[5] Antony J. Blinken, "The Administration's Approach to the People's Republic of China," speech delivered at George Washington University, Asia Society, May 26, 2022; "China to Defend Fairness and Justice in the Multilateral Arena: FM," Xinhua, December 30, 2021.

such strategy would be to generally weaken the ability and resolve of the United States to prevent China's eclipse while deterring the United States from resorting to armed force. Drawing from prior published RAND research, we outline several plausible victory conditions for any Chinese strategy to outcompete the United States. To be clear, these are assessed conditions, not goals that the Chinese government has stated publicly. However, no authoritative sources contradict these posited conditions. Moreover, our purpose in presenting them in this research is first and foremost to provide a baseline from which our analysis of specific PLA missions and tasks can proceed.

Our assessed victory conditions for Chinese competitive efforts against the United States, as established in prior RAND research, are as follows:

- War with the United States is avoided, although this condition does not exclude the possibility of militarized crises.
- The United States respects China's authority as the global leader, even as the United States remains a powerful but clearly inferior nation.
- The United States largely refrains from harming Chinese interests.
- China has established primacy across much of Eurasia, the Middle East, and Africa, principally through collaboration with a network of client states.
- U.S. primacy has been reduced to the Americas, although the United States might still maintain a military, economic, and diplomatic presence worldwide. Its alliances have been severely weakened or discontinued, especially in the Indo-Pacific.
- The United States and China manage their differences and cooperate according to norms upheld by China.[6]

In this chapter, we use this set of assessed victory conditions as a starting point for analyzing potential Chinese military missions and tasks to outcompete the United States.

China's Military Strategy to Outcompete the United States

China's pursuit of national revival relies heavily on the appeal of its economic power and diplomatic engagement. The ambitious BRI, which aims to integrate the Eurasian landmass through a China-led infrastructure and trade initiative, exemplifies China's approach.[7] In its competition with the United States, China also relies considerably on the appeal of its markets and efforts to build diplomatic partners in the developing world and the Indo-Pacific to gain a strategic advantage.

---

[6] These success criteria were first developed in Heath, Grossman, and Clark, 2019, p. xv, and remain applicable and relevant to this research's efforts to develop a list of PLA competition missions.

[7] Andrew Scobell, Edmund J. Burke, Cortez A. Cooper III, Sale Lilly, Chad J. R. Ohlandt, Eric Warner, J. D. Williams, *China's Grand Strategy*, RAND Corporation, RR-2798-A, 2020.

Military competition plays an important role as well. Chinese authorities have made clear that economic primacy in the Indo-Pacific is inadequate and that Beijing ultimately aspires to displace the United States as the primary security partner for most countries throughout the Indo-Pacific.[8] Chinese authorities have also identified virtually all elements of policy as carrying important security dimensions, which suggests that Beijing regards the military as playing a critical role in any competitive strategy.[9] As with the broader competitive strategy, we postulate that China's military competitive strategy likely consists of both a defensive effort to protect Chinese interests and an offensive effort that aims to weaken and erode U.S. capacity and will to prevent China's rise. In the following sections, we focus our analysis on PLA missions and tasks that we assess to be plausible and likely components of any Chinese strategy to outcompete the United States.

China's Military Strategic Missions

Since 2004, to help achieve the China Dream, Chinese leadership has assigned a set of missions or strategic responsibilities to the PLA known as the *historic missions*. The four historic missions call on the military to (1) ensure CCP rule, (2) protect China's territorial and sovereignty interests and national unity, (3) protect overseas interests, and (4) shape a favorable international order. These missions outline the military's role in protecting the core interests that Chinese leaders judge as essential to the country's survival and development.[10] As we use the terms, military *missions* consist of the broad strategic responsibilities that link military *tasks* to whole-of-government national goals and strategies. As a result, we start with these historic missions as a first step in deriving tasks that the PLA is likely to execute in peacetime competition campaigns.

China's government has not published any set of more-specific missions for the PLA in support of competition with the United States. These historic missions are directives to protect the core interests regarded by Chinese authorities as vital to realizing the China Dream.[11] These core interests, as developed by Chinese officials, include interests related to political security and social stability, sovereignty and territory, economic development, and the international security environment.[12] China's security policy, which includes missions assigned to the military, fundamentally focuses on these core interests. For the purposes of our analysis, we translate these core interests and their underlying new historic missions into four discrete objectives for the CCP and PLA in competition with the United States: (1) political and social

---

[8] State Council Information Office, 2017.

[9] Xi Jinping, "A Holistic View of National Security," *Qiushi*, December 4, 2020.

[10] State Council Information Office, 2019.

[11] China's core interests face threats from sources other than those associated with the United States, of course, but these are not dealt with in this report. This research focuses on the mission sets directly applicable to competition and conflict scenarios involving the United States and its allies and partners.

[12] State Council Information Office, 2019.

stability internal to China, (2) basic security, national sovereignty, and the territorial integrity of China, (3) protection of overseas Chinese interests, and (4) international influence, partnerships, and pro-Chinese narratives abroad.[13]

To facilitate more-detailed analysis, we decompose each of the hypothesized Chinese core interests into pairs of defensive and offensive missions (Table 2.1). *Defensive missions* are those efforts undertaken by the PLA to protect Chinese core interests from externally backed threats. *Offensive missions* are the efforts undertaken by the PLA to weaken or threaten the analogous vital national interests of the United States and its allies and partners.[14]

These strategic missions cover the breadth of military activity that directly support the broader whole-of-government strategy to outcompete the United States. Successful execution of these missions will not alone ensure that China prevailed over the United States, because much would depend on Beijing's management of the economic and diplomatic dimensions of the contest. However, a successful military competition would mitigate one of the United States' greatest competitive strengths—the credibility and appeal of its military power. Successful execution of a military competitive strategy could also significantly increase the appeal of Chinese international leadership and thus provide an important advantage.

Because these missions are supporting peacetime competition, they do not involve any kinetic actions against U.S. forces. Rather, they consist of nonwar operations, actions, and activities designed to generally strengthen China's strategic position and weaken that of the

TABLE 2.1

People's Liberation Army Peacetime Missions to Support China's Competition with the United States

Core Interests	Defensive Missions	Offensive Missions
Political and social stability	Defensive Mission 1: Defend CCP rule and social stability from externally backed threats	Offensive Mission 1: Prepare options to threaten the political legitimacy, and social stability of U.S. allies and partners, such as Taiwan
Basic security, national sovereignty, territorial integrity	Defensive Mission 2: Deter externally backed threats to China's basic security, sovereignty, territorial integrity	Offensive Mission 2: Secure disputed territory controlled by U.S. allies and partners through nonkinetic methods
Overseas interests	Defensive Mission 3: Deter potential externally backed threats to overseas interests	Offensive Mission 3: Prepare options to damage U.S. and allied overseas interests
International influence, partnerships, and narrative	Defensive Mission 4: Defend Chinese influence, access, and partnerships from externally backed malign influence	Offensive Mission 4: Weaken and undermine U.S. influence, access, and alliances and partnerships

SOURCES: Features information from Heath, Grossman, and Clark, 2021; and Heath, Gunness, and Finazzo, 2022.

---

[13] These objectives are adapted from the CCP Defense Strategy Mission framework in Heath, Grossman, and Clark, 2021, p. 64.

[14] This definition follows the approach taken in prior RAND research focused on low-intensity conflict missions for the PLA. See Heath Gunness, and Finazzo, 2022, p. 94.

United States and its allies. Chinese execution of these offensive missions must also be sensitive to the escalation risks of posing too great a threat to any adversary's core interests.

Defensive Mission 1 focuses on efforts to ensure political and social stability within China and directs the PLA to carry out activities to deter and defeat any externally backed effort to undermine the legitimacy of CCP rule and social stability. Defensive Mission 2 focuses on efforts to ensure territorial sovereignty and calls on the PLA to defend against potential physical threats backed by external actors against Chinese territory, including Tibet and Xinjiang, Taiwan, the South China Sea, and the East China Sea. Defensive Mission 3 focuses on efforts to protect overseas interests and directs the PLA to deter potential externally backed threats to China's broad array of overseas interests. Defensive Mission 4 focuses on efforts to defend against malign influence abroad, and calls on the PLA to protect and deter externally backed threats to Chinese influence, access, narratives, and partnerships worldwide.

Offensive Mission 1 also focuses on an adversary's core interests in political and social stability and requires the PLA to prepare options to foment social instability or challenge the political legitimacy of U.S. allies and partners, including Taiwan. Offensive Mission 2 concerns an adversary's core interests of territory and sovereignty. In this case, the mission principally involves the territory and sovereignty of key U.S. allies and partners located near China's periphery. This mission requires the PLA to secure contested territory from relevant U.S. allies and partners through primarily nonwar methods, such as law enforcement, legal warfare, and economic coercion. Offensive Mission 3 focuses on overseas interests and tasks the PLA with preparing options to threaten those overseas interests, such as military facilities and digital infrastructure of the United States and its allies and partners. Offensive Mission 4 focuses on adversary core interests related to influence and access and directs the PLA to carry out various operations, activities, and investments to weaken, erode, and undermine U.S. influence, access, narratives, and alliances and partnerships abroad.

To translate these broad missions into discrete military activities for the purposes of this report, the remainder of this chapter provides a more detailed analysis of potential PLA tasks to support each PLA mission required to enable China's broader strategy to outcompete the United States. We define *tasks* as specific work assigned to the military for the purpose of fulfilling one or more of the PLA's strategic missions. In the subsequent sections of this chapter, we derive and analyze the specific tasks associated with each mission, the types of military forces that could be involved, relevant nonmilitary assets that could be involved, and the most-relevant geographic regions where the task applies. We also analyze potential vulnerabilities that Chinese military forces might face in attempting to implement the tasks.

People's Liberation Army Defensive Missions in Peacetime Competition

We begin by deriving a series of tasks associated with each of the PLA's four defensive missions to outcompete the United States, analyzing the PLA's likely execution of these tasks, and assessing potential vulnerabilities in its ability to achieve Beijing's strategic objectives.

Defensive Mission 1: Defend Chinese Communist Party Rule and Social Stability from Externally Backed Threats

In Defensive Mission 1, the central leadership directs the PLA to protect the CCP and China's social stability from potential externally backed threats that might arise during U.S.-China peacetime competition. The CCP regards the perpetuation of its rule as the most essential of the military's responsibilities, and critical to that goal are efforts to ensure domestic peace and stability. This mission applies specifically to the Chinese mainland, or Region 1 in our geographic laydown of PLA missions and roles.

We assess that there are two principal tasks for this mission, both of which are focused on efforts to control potential external-influence threats to domestic populations within China (Table 2.2).

As a part of Task 1, the PLA supports civilian authorities in deterring and defeating potential externally backed challenges to CCP rule in ethnically Han–dominated regions. Beijing has always been suspicious of alleged U.S. and European efforts to instigate "color revolu-

TABLE 2.2
People's Liberation Army Tasks to Defend Chinese Communist Party Rule, Social Stability from Externally Backed Threats (Peacetime Competition Defensive Mission 1)

PLA Task	Chinese Forces	Execution	Coordination with Nonmilitary Assets
Task 1: Control externally backed threats to ethnically Han–dominated areas	• PAP • PLAGF • PAFM • PLASSF	• PAP augments law enforcement in suppressing popular challenges to CCP rule • PLA intelligence supports surveillance, monitoring	• Civilian intelligence and security services • CAC • Provincial governments
Task 2: Control externally backed threats to ethnic-minority areas	• PAP • PLAGF • PAFM • PLASSF	• PAP augments law enforcement to suppress separatist activity; counterterrorism operations • PLA intelligence, surveillance, and reconnaissance (ISR) helps monitor separatist groups	• Civilian intelligence and security services • Counterterrorism law enforcement units • CAC • Provincial governments

NOTE: PAFM = People's Armed Forces Militia

tions" against authoritarian regimes around the world.[15] In this context, China and the PLA seek to prevent externally backed activists and agitators from leading a rebellion against the CCP itself. This task builds on Chinese fears of foreign agents. During the Hong Kong protests in 2019, for example, the CCP labeled protesters as foreign agents and terrorists to justify its harsh responses.[16]

In terms of PLA efforts to execute this task, we assess that Beijing would rely on the PAP and PAFM to control crowds internal to China. In more-severe cases, the PLAGF could be used to intervene and crush large-scale uprisings that exceeded the capacity of the PAP. The PLASSF could also be employed to provide necessary intelligence support to these operations. However, these military units would primarily be used to augment the civilian security and intelligence services that are responsible for ensuring public order. Other nonmilitary assets could include provincial governments, propaganda-media, and censorship offices that would promote pro-regime messages and suppress dissenting views within mainland China.

A potential vulnerability in the PLA's execution of this task is the danger of disobedience or politicization in the military in carrying out domestic stability operations. In the Tiananmen Square massacre, for example, some units refused to carry out orders to fire on the civilian populace. Alarmed by the reports of insubordination, Chinese leaders subsequently redirected the PLA away from domestic security missions.[17] A related reason for this change was to reduce the danger that factions or other rival elites within the CCP might try to direct elements of the PLA to contend for power, which happened in the violent power struggles of the Cultural Revolution.[18] Chinese leadership concerns about ensuring the loyalty of the military executing domestic security duties could hamper the ability of PLA units to effectively support this task.

The PLA's second task under this broader mission would be to control potential externally backed separatist threats to the legitimacy of CCP rule in ethnic minority–dominated regions within China. China has been primarily concerned about maintaining the security and stability of its restive western provinces, Tibet and Xinjiang. These provinces are the home of large numbers of ethnic minorities, Tibetans and Uighurs respectively, two groups that have experienced considerable discrimination and maltreatment by the Han-dominated government. The Inner Mongolia province features another important minority group, the Hui people, that has experienced similar treatment.[19] Beijing's fear of separatism has prompted

---

[15] "Russia, China Oppose Color Revolutions—Joint Statement," TASS, February 4, 2022.

[16] Steven Lee Myers, "In Hong Kong Protests, China Angrily Connects Dots Back to U.S.," *New York Times*, November 30, 2020.

[17] Timothy Brook, *Quelling the People: The Military Suppression of the Beijing Democracy Movement*, Oxford University Press, 1992.

[18] Harvey Nelsen, "Military Forces in the Cultural Revolution," *China Quarterly*, Vol. 51, July 1972.

[19] Emily Feng, "'Afraid We Will Become the Next Xinjiang:' China's Hui Muslims Face Crackdown," NPR, September 26, 2019; Antonio Graceffo, "China's Crackdown on Mongolian Culture," *The Diplomat*, September 4, 2020.

it to take extreme actions against minority groups, ranging from *Hanification*, eliminating their culture and absorbing them into the Han race, to jailing them in concentration camps.[20] Beijing already judges that external actors are involved in fomenting unrest in these sensitive regions, and it has accordingly directed PAP and militia forces to augment civilian security services in these regions.[21] Unlike the first task of this mission, we expect that the PAP anti-terrorist units would play a larger role in suppressing perceived separatist activities.

One possible vulnerability in China's execution of these tasks would be the risk that military violence to suppress protests could accelerate unrest and aggravate dissatisfaction with CCP rule. Specifically, heavy-handed responses from Beijing's security forces could result in escalating violence that results in casualties to bystanders. Continued repression could also result in lost economic opportunities for Chinese companies and damage to China's international reputation, including in the global South. Already, international condemnation of the repression has resulted in economic losses for companies tied to repressive policies.[22] Criticism of Chinese repression has also increased around the world, including in some Muslim countries.[23] Anger at the reported abuses could also motivate radicalized groups to take violent action against China.

Defensive Mission 2: Deter Externally Backed Threats to China's Basic Security, Sovereignty, and Territorial Integrity

The second defensive mission for the PLA in competition with the United States concerns the protection of basic national security, territorial integrity, and sovereignty within Chinese territory. This mission involves the general task of ensuring the integrity of Chinese borders and sovereign control over all claimed territory against external threats and the politically sensitive task of ensuring national unity through the eventual recovery of Taiwan. The focus on the political integrity of China's borders distinguishes this mission from Defensive Mission 1, which mostly concerns social and political stability within Chinese territory. Moreover, China regards its cyberspace as "sovereign territory," and security for its cyber networks also falls under this mission.[24] In terms of the geographic focus of the PLA's activities to execute this mission, China's leadership would likely task the PLA with deterring potential externally backed threats to its basic security, sovereignty, and territorial integrity within China and along its borders, or Region 1 in our geographic laydown.

---

[20] "Who Are the Uyghurs and Why Is China Being Accused of Genocide?" BBC News, June 21, 2021.

[21] Dibyesh Anand, "Colonization with Chinese Characteristics: Politics of (In)security in Xinjiang and Tibet," *Asian Survey*, Vol. 38, No. 1, 2019.

[22] "U.S. Adds 14 Chinese Companies to Economic Blacklist Over Xinjiang," Reuters, July 10, 2021.

[23] "More Countries Criticize China at UN for Repression of Uighurs," *Al Jazeera*, October 22, 2021.

[24] Adam Segal, *China's Vision for Cyber Sovereignty and the Global Governance of Cyberspace*, National Bureau of Asian Research, August 25, 2020.

TABLE 2.3

People's Liberation Army Tasks to Deter Externally Backed Threats to China's Basic Security, Sovereignty, and Territorial Integrity (Peacetime Competition Defensive Mission 2)

PLA Task	Chinese Forces	Execution	Coordination with Nonmilitary Assets
Task 1: Deter potential U.S. threats to homeland	• PLASSF • PLARF • PLAN • PLAAF • PLA SOF	• PLASSF carries out deterrence and response operations against potential nuclear, conventional, cyber, and space threats	• Civilian intelligence and security services • UFWD
Task 2: Deter potential externally backed threats to China's sovereign territory	• PLAGF • PLAAF • PLASSF • PAP • CCG	• PLA patrols border regions and ensures readiness to defeat any incursion or attack on maritime and land borders	• Civilian intelligence and security services • Provincial governments • MFA • UFWD
Task 3: Deter Taiwan from externally backed separatist activity	• PLA (all services)	• PLA maintains readiness to defeat any externally backed separatist activity, demonstrates combat power, coerces Taiwan	• TAO • Civilian intelligence and security services • UFWD

We assess that this mission includes three principal tasks: deter potential U.S. threats to China's homeland, deter external threats from other actors to China's border regions, and deter externally backed separatist activity in Taiwan (Table 2.3).

The PLA's first task in this mission is to deter potential territorial threats to the Chinese homeland from the United States and its allies and partners. PLA forces are likely to play a key role in backstopping diplomatic messages and ensuring readiness to support this task. The PLARF plays a critical role in deterring potential U.S. nuclear attack with their own missile forces.[25] A related threat lies in deterring the risk of conventional strikes against the Chinese mainland. Beijing has spent decades steadily building out its anti-access area denial capabilities in the form of longer-ranging ballistic and cruise missiles, surface and subsurface fleets, and bomber and fighter wings in large part to extend its defensive depth and reduce the risks of such strikes in conflict. The likelihood of nuclear or conventional attacks occurring against the Chinese mainland in peacetime is extremely low, yet it remains a peacetime competition mission for the PLA to deter any such attack.[26] The PLA is likely to coordinate its preparedness message through the MFA and propaganda-media channels.

The PLA is also involved in deterrence in the cyber and space domains, each of which are active in peacetime competition. There is evidence to suggest that China views attacks on its

---

[25] John Costello and Joe McReynolds, in Philip C. Saunders, Arthur S. Ding, Andrew Scobell, Andrew N. D. Yang, and Joel Wuthnow, eds., *Chairman Xi Remakes the PLA: Assessing Chinese Military Reforms*, National Defense University Press, 2019, p. 37.

[26] M. Taylor Fravel, *China's Military Strategy Since 1949: Active Defense*, Princeton University Press, 2019.

cyber networks as violations of its sovereignty. Chinese authorities argue that the country has the sovereign right to organize and manage its cyber networks, and they maintain that no other country has the right to interfere with those networks.[27] Intrusions or attacks could be met in kind with retaliatory cyber measures by the PLA, even during peacetime. The Joint Staff Department's Network Security Defense Center units work closely with civilian counterparts, including the CAC, to ensure defense of China's cyber networks.[28]

China similarly regards potential U.S. attacks on its space systems as a violation of its space sovereignty. Chinese authorities explain that Beijing has the sovereign right to manage its space assets and sensors and that no country has the right to interfere with its space assets.[29] Attacks on Chinese space assets would likely be met with in-kind responses. The PLASSF manages deterrence of threats in the space domain and has developed a variety of antispace weapons as deterrents to such aggression. The PLARF also plays a role in this deterrence with its antisatellite missile capabilities.[30]

Although the PLA's homeland defense missions to ensure basic national security remain paramount, there are several vulnerabilities in the execution of these tasks. One danger is the risk of unintended escalation, especially in the cyber domain, in which attribution is often difficult to establish. Chinese desires to retaliate for perceived violations of its cyber sovereignty could result in miscalculations that inadvertently escalate a limited dispute into a larger conflict. This possibility could create hesitancy on the part of Chinese decisionmakers to respond aggressively, or it could create potential blowback against China if its responses were seen as disproportionate. Another vulnerability lies in the aggravation of threat perceptions that could accompany China's efforts to deter potential violations of its territorial, cyber, and space sovereignty. China's launching of antisatellite missiles in 2007, for example, fueled fears of Chinese intentions to militarize space.[31] Similarly, China's construction of large numbers of missile silos to enhance nuclear deterrence intensified concerns about China's strategic intentions.[32]

The second task under this broader defensive mission is to deter potential externally backed threats to China's land, air, and maritime sovereign territory along its physical borders. This task principally concerns potential disputes in the East and South China seas and border areas with India. In terms of military forces, deterrence of potential incursions of

---

[27] "Chinese Envoy Urges Formulating International Rules for Cyberspace Generally Accepted by All Nations," Xinhua, June 30, 2021.

[28] Costello and McReynolds, 2019.

[29] Krista Langeland and Derek Grossman, *Tailoring Deterrence for China in Space*, RAND Corporation, RR-A943-1, 2021, pp. 27–28.

[30] Pollpeter, Chase, and Heginbotham, 2017.

[31] Sandra Erwin, "Pentagon Report: China Amassing Arsenal of Anti-Satellite Weapons," *SpaceNews*, September 1, 2020.

[32] Steven Lee Myers, "China Bolsters Its Nuclear Options with New Missile Silos in a Desert," *New York Times*, July 2, 2021.

land borders involves the PLAGF, PLAAF, PLASSF, and PAP. These ground forces train and prepare options to counter incursions and reclaim territory seized by rivals. At sea, Beijing relies primarily on all military services, the CCG, and the PAFMM to carry out deterrence. China also regards U.S. air and maritime patrols along its border regions as threatening. Enhanced deterrence could include additional PLA patrols of border regions to ensure readiness to defeat any incursion or attack on maritime and land borders. Nonmilitary assets would likely consist of civilian intelligence, provincial governments, security services, the MFA, and the UFWD.

A vulnerability in China's deterrence of threats to border areas lies in the potential for undue escalation from overly aggressive tactics to enforce its sovereign claims in disputed areas. Miscalculation in the PLA's execution of operations to defend border areas could aggravate threat perceptions as well, contributing to a worsening of China's security environment. China's brawl with India in 2020, for example, resulted in the deaths of at least 20 soldiers and likely fueled India's growing cooperation with the United States through involvement in the Quadrilateral Security Dialogue.[33]

The third task of this mission is for the PLA to deter externally backed Taiwan forces that support formal independence. This task involves all PLA services, although their role in peacetime rests solely on preparing for potential future operations and signaling the PLA's warfighting capabilities that are specific to Taiwan reunification as a deterrent to potential U.S. intervention if such a conflict were to occur. The PLA's most essential work for this task consists of preparations to carry out combat operations to prevent the island's formal independence and forcibly reintegrate Taiwan. The PLAN, in conjunction with the CCG and PAFMM, could also prepare a blockade or amphibious landing against Taiwan. In August 2022, PLA forces executed a drill simulating a blockade in response to U.S. Speaker of the House Nancy Pelosi's visit to Taiwan.[34] The PLAGF can train and prepare for an invasion of Taiwan, and the PLARF can train and prepare for a joint missile strike against the island. The PLASSF would support these operations with cyber, ISR, and information operations. Military forces, such as the TAO and the CCP's UFWD, and civilian intelligence and security services provide the backbone to civilian-led efforts to deter separatism and encourage unification.

A major vulnerability for the PLA in its peacetime ability to support Taiwan reunification lies in the limited effectiveness of military nonkinetic options. Although the PLA can certainly demonstrate its combat power as a means of intimidating Taiwan and deterring U.S. intervention in a potential conflict, these efforts are just as likely to harden Taiwan's resolve to resist Chinese demands for peaceful unification. Repression within China, especially in regions such as Xinjiang and Hong Kong, has further driven the Taiwanese populace away

---

[33] Jeffrey Gettleman, "Anger Surges in India over Deadly Border Brawl with China," *New York Times*, June 18, 2020.

[34] Cyril Ip, "Chinese PLA Drills Simulating Taiwan Blockade Seen to Become 'New Normal,'" *South China Morning Post*, August 9, 2022.

from the idea of unification, and the range of influence and information operations directed against Taiwan has done little to build goodwill toward China. On the contrary, polls suggest that the people of Taiwan have grown overwhelmingly opposed to unification.[35] Another vulnerability lies in the risk of escalation from the PLA's attempts to coerce the island through limited force short of war. The PLA's real combat abilities remain untested, and its ability to successfully convey sufficient troops across the Taiwan Strait in combat conditions remains unclear.[36] The final vulnerability lies in the drain on resources from the PLA's high pace of operations and activities near the island. These activities could draw resources away from deterrence and missions in other theaters.

Defensive Mission 3: Deter Potential Externally Backed Threats to Overseas Interests

The third set of missions involves defending China's overseas interests from externally backed threats. Many Chinese workers are employed abroad, often in developing countries with internal instability. This especially true for China's presence in fragile BRI countries.[37] China has little reason to view the United States specifically as a military threat to its overseas interests, but a deepening of hostility in U.S.-China competition could raise Beijing's concern about the vulnerability of its overseas assets. The PLA would likely conduct this mission outside China and the United States, in Regions 2 and 3 in our geographic laydown.

This mission would likely entail two main tasks: deter externally backed threats against Chinese overseas interests and provide military assistance to friendly foreign governments to protect China's overseas interests (Table 2.4).

The first task directs the PLA to deter potential externally backed threats to overseas assets and citizens. In peacetime, the main threats to Chinese overseas interests are likely to stem from nontraditional sources, such as violent nonstate actors. However, Chinese military forces could be used to step up intelligence collection on nearby U.S. forces to monitor potential threats. To deter and respond to attacks on Chinese infrastructure and citizens overseas, China relies primarily on state-run PSCs and host-nation military and security forces, with PLA forces playing a supporting role in extreme circumstances.[38] PSCs play a key role through intelligence collection, reconnaissance, training, and escort duties for Chinese civilians abroad.[39] If the lives of Chinese nationals are at risk, particularly in a crisis, then the PLA

---

[35] John Feng, "Taiwan's Desire for Unification with China Near Record Low as Tensions Rise," *Newsweek*, July 14, 2022.

[36] Joel Wuthnow, Derek Grossman, Philip C. Saunders, Andrew Scobell, and Andrew N. D. Yang, *Crossing the Strait*, National Defense University Press, 2022.

[37] Hillman and Tippett, 2021.

[38] Nadège Rolland, ed., *Securing the Belt and Road Initiative: China's Evolving Military Engagement Along the Silk Roads*, National Bureau of Asian Research, September 3, 2019.

[39] Jingdong, 2022.

TABLE 2.4

People's Liberation Army Tasks to Deter Potential Externally Backed Threats to Overseas Interests (Peacetime Competition Defensive Mission 3)

PLA Task	Chinese Forces	Execution	Coordination with Nonmilitary Assets
Task 1: Deter externally backed threats against overseas assets and citizens	• PLA (all services)	• PLA operations where feasible to control threats; coordinate with PSCs and host-nation militaries as needed to protect Chinese assets	• MFA • PMC • Host-nation militaries and security forces
Task 2: Provide military assistance to protect client state assets and citizens from externally backed threats	• PMC • PLA technicians and advisers	• Conduct intelligence sharing, combined exercises, joint patrols, arms sales to help partner control threats	• MFA • PMC • Host-nation militaries and security forces

might be directed to conduct a noncombatant evacuation operation (NEO) or search-and-rescue (SAR) operation leveraging the same forces detailed above. The MFA is likely to play an important role in coordinating political and military related tasks between China and host countries both in steady-state competition and in a potential crisis requiring PLA involvement in NEO or SAR efforts.

A vulnerability in China's execution of this task is the limited experience, capability, and posture of PLA military forces to carry out such operations abroad. China has only one overseas military base, located in Djibouti. Its military forces have experienced overseas operations only under largely noncombat conditions, principally as part of United Nations peacekeeping missions.[40] Although its access to facilities could grow in the future, it seems unlikely that China will ever build a network of military bases as robust as the United States' network because Beijing has shown little interest in developing the sorts of alliances and security obligations that could grant them such basing access. Rather, authorities seem intent on establishing logistics supply points to provide opportunities for replenishment for passing ships and aircraft.[41] Chinese leaders are aware of these limitations, and the PLA has accordingly increased the size of its deployable marine corps, ocean-going naval ships, and long-distance transport aircraft, improving the PLA's ability to operate abroad.[42] However, in the event of a crisis abroad that involves Chinese nationals or infrastructure, the possibility that China's military could prove incapable of defending its own people in a very public manner could

---

[40] State Council Information Office, 2019.

[41] Nathan Beauchamp Mustafaga, "Where to Next? PLA Considerations for Overseas Base Selection," *China Brief,* Vol. 20, No. 18, October 19, 2020.

[42] Rolland, p. 4.

lead the Chinese government to rethink some of its lesser priority overseas commitments in the future.

The second task under this peacetime competition mission directs the PLA to provide military assistance to partner nations that host Chinese assets and citizens. With this task, China seeks to promote friendly military-to-military relationships with would-be partner nations abroad, mainly through arms sales and training. China has significantly increased arms sales to partner nations, such as Nigeria and Iran.[43] Chinese military forces also train with such partners as Russia and Iran.[44]

A vulnerability in this task lies in the danger that Chinese support for a partner could worsen threat perceptions of Chinese intent in specific regions abroad and possibly drag Beijing into unintended conflicts not of its own choosing. Russia attempted to extract specific military support from China during its invasion of Ukraine in 2022, for example. Although China resisted such demands, its reputation nonetheless suffered in Western countries as China was cast as an enabler of Russian aggression.[45]

A broader vulnerability for both tasks under this mission is that PLA failures to effectively secure Chinese interests abroad might constrain China's ability to assert its influence in potential client states that are looking for help with internal security threats. Evidence that China could not materially help a client state cope with its security problems could open opportunities for competitors, such as the United States, to offer military aid in China's stead. Another vulnerability lies in the potential for Chinese embarrassment, failures, or casualties in operations abroad. Chinese military forces have acted with considerable caution and the CCP's cultivation of its image as a helpful, competent force could incentivize it to avoid operations and actions that carry too high a risk of failure or embarrassment. In China's counter-piracy missions in the 2010s, for example, China generally shied away from conducting risky rescue operations that might result in military casualties. Authorities have often instead paid ransom demands, perhaps in part because of recognition of the limits of PLA capabilities.[46] To date, Beijing has also been sensitive to the potential for casualties in military operations abroad. After its clash with Indian forces in 2020 along the Aksai Chin border region between the two countries, Chinese authorities suppressed discussion of the Chinese casualties, and the true number of deaths from that incident remains unclear.[47]

---

[43] Jacob Parakilas, "The China-US Arms Trade Arms Race," *The Diplomat*, August 6, 2021.

[44] Kenneth Allen, Philip C. Saunders, and John Chen, *Chinese Military Diplomacy 2003–2016: Trends and Implications*, National Defense University Press, July 17, 2017.

[45] Joshua Kurlantzick, "China's Already Poor Global Image Is Being Hurt by Ukraine War," *Asia Unbound*, blog, Council for Foreign Relations, March 24, 2022.

[46] Andrew Erickson and Austin Strange, *No Substitute for Experience: Chinese Anti-Piracy Operations in the Gulf of Aden*, Naval War College, November 2013.

[47] Emily Feng, "China Makes It a Crime to Question Military Casualties on the Internet," *NPR*, March 22, 2021.

Defensive Mission 4: Defend Chinese Influence, Access, and Partnerships from External-Backed Malign Influence

The fourth defensive mission concerns the protection of Chinese influence, access, and partnerships from externally backed threats. As China's global interests continue to grow, the PLA has increased its involvement in military diplomacy with counterpart nations.[48] Indeed, this mission fundamentally centers on the protection of Chinese diplomatic and military relationships with partners around the world as an influence mechanism to promote Chinese interests. This mission applies to all regions outside China and the United States, or Regions 2 and 3 in our geographic laydown.

There are two main tasks for the PLA to execute in this mission: counter U.S. actions that subvert China's influence in specific countries abroad and counter U.S. actions that subvert China's broader narrative globally (Table 2.5).

In the first task, the PLA counters U.S. efforts to undermine Chinese influence, access, and partnerships by building its own partnerships with key countries abroad. Chinese military attachés, which are now present in 130 countries, would play a key role in this task.[49] Relevant activities for the PLA could include routinized military or defense dialogues with partner nations, arms sales, port visits, combined exercises, trainings, and visits by senior-level military leadership.[50] Such military diplomatic activities allow the PLA to learn about foreign militaries and improve their own operational capabilities while strengthening Chinese ties to key partner states.[51] The PLAN, PAP, PLAGF, and PLAAF all participate in grow-

TABLE 2.5

People's Liberation Army Tasks to Defend Chinese Influence, Access, and Partnerships from U.S. Malign Influence Abroad (Peacetime Competition Defensive Mission 4)

PLA Task	Chinese Forces	Execution	Coordination: Nonmilitary Assets
Task 1: Counter U.S. efforts to undermine China's influence, access, partnerships	• PLA (all services) • PAP	• PLA officials pressure host nations to downgrade U.S. access, influence as a condition for Chinese benefits	• MFA • UFWD • Propaganda-media
Task 2: Counter U.S. efforts to undermine China's global narrative	• PLASSF	• PLA specialists support civilian propaganda, messaging	• MFA • UFWD • Propaganda-media

---

[48] China Power Team, "How Is China Bolstering Its Military Diplomatic Relations?" ChinaPower, Center for Strategic and International Studies, August 26, 2020.

[49] State Council Information Office of the People's Republic of China, 2019.

[50] Allen, Saunders, and Chen, 2017.

[51] Richard Weitz, "Assessing Chinese-Russian Military Exercises: Past Progress and Future Trends," Center for Strategic and International Studies, July 2021.

ing numbers of such exchanges with a variety of partner nations. China is also a growing arms exporter to a variety of states.[52] These exports are often accompanied by the temporary dispatch of PLA or civilian trainers to build the capacity of recipient military forces to operate Chinese-exported equipment.[53] These military tasks would augment civilian efforts led by the MFA, the UFWD, and propaganda-media organizations to promote Chinese influence in key regions.

The second task under this mission calls on the PLA to support the Chinese government's efforts to counter global U.S. messaging activities that undermine China's influence and global narrative. This task is a long-standing CCP objective, well embodied in the PLA's "Three Warfares" doctrine. The Three Warfares doctrine calls on the military to carry out media, psychological, and legal influence operations.[54] For this task, Beijing is likely to instruct the PLASSF to conduct cyber and intelligence operations in support of activities by state-run propaganda-media, the MFA, and the UFWD, targeting populations in specific countries abroad with anti-U.S. messages, and feeding pro-Chinese narratives into the information environment.

A possible vulnerability in China's execution of these tasks lies in the limited ability of Chinese military forces to promote positive perceptions of China among local populations and civil society leaders and to promote enduring diplomatic alliances and relationships that span multiple dimensions of national power, not just military alliances and relationships. The limited Chinese success in extending its influence throughout the world also owes to constraints arising from the PLA's facility in foreign languages. Until 1997, the PLA's University of Foreign Languages, which teaches foreign languages to military personnel, only offered 11 languages. That number grew to 26 languages by 2011, including English, Hindi, Nepali, Lao, Thai, and Russian. By contrast the U.S. military's Defense Language Institute teaches 40 languages,[55] and the U.S. military has decades of experience operating in countries around the world. By one 2021 estimate , the United States had 750 bases located in at least 80 countries worldwide.[56] By contrast, China's military presence in countries along BRI routes is relatively modest and recent. Broad-based ties between countries are often forged for political, cultural, and geographic reasons over many years, and China's limited military engagement abroad limits the potential for developing such ties in the same manner that the United States has.

---

[52] Joshua Chang, "China's Arms Diplomacy in Venezuela Affects Stability in the Western Hemisphere," *Georgetown Security Studies Review*, October 27, 2020; April Herlevi, "China as a Niche Arms Exporter," Centers for Naval Analysis, August 31, 2021.

[53] Samy Akil and Karam Shaar, *The Red Dragon in the Land of Jasmine: An Overview of China's Role in the Syrian Conflict*, Operations and Policy Center, March 24, 2021.

[54] Peter Mattis, "China's 'Three Warfares' in Perspective," *War on the Rocks*, January 30, 2018.

[55] Scott Henderson, "Polyglot Dragon," *Armed Forces Journal*, Vol. 149, No. 1, November 2011.

[56] Mohammed Hussein and Mohammed Haddad, "Infographic: US Military Presence Around the World," *Al Jazeera*, September 10, 2021.

A related vulnerability lies in China's approach to its own foreign policy, through which it seeks to cultivate positive relations with all countries where feasible and avoid getting mired in regional disputes. As a result, China has to carefully balance its diplomatic efforts to avoid taking sides in disputes amongst its potential partners. Beijing's efforts to cultivate ties with both Iran and Saudi Arabia, for example, constrains its willingness to sell arms or bolster security ties with either side. Such diplomatic constraints result in a relatively shallow relationship with many countries and in turn likely limit how much partner states might be willing to sacrifice for the sake of China's desire to avoid taking sides.

Many countries choose to engage with China for economic benefits but resist a closer military relationship with the PLA. The nature of these relationships could open opportunities for China's competitors to maintain military access and influence along China's periphery, even where Chinese economic influence is predominant. It also raises the risk that Chinese frustrations over the inability to translate economic and diplomatic leverage into military partnerships could drive coercive behaviors, which might further alienate host nations.

PLA Offensive Missions in Peacetime Competition

In this section, we review the tasks associated with each of the four offensive missions that the PLA might be expected to carry out in peacetime competition with the United States. Because these are peacetime missions, they do not involve kinetic strikes or lethal activities. Rather, they consist of nonkinetic actions to harm U.S. influence and access. They also involve preparations for kinetic options in the event of escalation into conflict or potential escalation into a more hostile state of competition. In all cases, offensive peacetime competition missions include more-direct efforts to weaken U.S. influence, partnerships, and access abroad as potential impediments to the realization of the China Dream.

Offensive Mission 1: Prepare Options to Threaten the Political Legitimacy, Social Stability of the United States and its Allies and Partners

The first offensive mission is for the PLA to develop options to threaten the political legitimacy and social stability of the United States or its allies and partners, primarily in the Indo-Pacific. China actively carries out efforts to destabilize Taiwan's government through information operations and other political activities.[57] But outside the cross-strait dispute, little evidence exists to suggest that China is carrying out missions to destabilize governments or foment significant social unrest in the United States or any of its other allies and partners. However, an aggravation of the competition with the United States could lead Beijing to

---

[57] Joyce Huang, "China Using 'Cognitive Warfare' Against Taiwan, Observers Say," *Voice of America,* January 17, 2021.

adopt more-aggressive tactics, especially if Beijing believed the United States to be conduct-ing similar actions against China. Such missions would likely occur either in the U.S. home-land (Region 4 in our geographic laydown) or would be primarily focused on U.S. allies and partners along China's periphery (Region 2).

We assess that there is one principal task for the PLA, summarized in Table 2.6, to pre-pare such options for threatening the legitimacy of China's competitors during peacetime competition. Authorities could direct the PLA to prepare options to provoke instability and popular discontent in the United States through cyber and informational means, following precedents set by Chinese interference in Taiwan's elections and Russian interference in U.S. elections. Alternatively, in a more hostile competition, China could direct the PLA to pro-mote similar unrest through cyber and informational means in the societies of U.S. allies and partners in the Indo-Pacific, such as Australia, Japan, and the Philippines. Evidence that the PLA might carry out such preparations can be seen in its interest in "cognitive domain opera-tions." According to PLA writings, such operations aim to prevail over an adversary without fighting by directly changing perceptions through actions in the physical, informational, and cognitive domains.[58]

The main point of such activity would be to keep the respective governments divided and distracted internally, thereby limiting their ability to focus on China in peacetime or in con-flict. Execution of this task would mainly involve PLASSF units that specialize in cyber and psychological operations and could carry out cognitive domain operations.[59] In areas along China's periphery, such as Taiwan, PLA SOF units could also play a role in preparing options for sabotage or other provocations intended to further domestic division in targeted societies. These military forces would cooperate with civilian intelligence and security services and the UFWD, which might pursue similar propaganda, solicitation, and other subversive activities. Such preparations could facilitate peacetime efforts to coerce targeted countries. To date, similar activities have been targeted against Taiwan, but they could be widened to be used

TABLE 2.6

People's Liberation Army Tasks to Prepare Options to Threaten the Political Legitimacy, Social Stability of the United States and its Allies and Partners (Peacetime Competition Offensive Mission 1)

PLA Task	Chinese Forces	Execution	Coordination with Nonmilitary Assets
Task 1: Prepare options to threaten the legitimacy and social stability of the United States and its key Asian allies and partners	• PLASSF • PLA SOF	• PLASSF units identify vulnerabilities in enemy cyber networks, information domains that can be targeted in wartime	• Civilian intelligence and security services • UFWD

[58] Koichiro Takagi, "The Future of China's Cognitive Domain Operations: Lessons from the War in Ukraine," *War on the Rocks*, July 22, 2022.

[59] Nathan Beauchamp-Mustafaga, "Cognitive Domain Operations," *China Brief*, Vol. 19, No. 16, Septem-ber 6, 2019.

against more countries in the future as conditions change in U.S.-China competition and in China's relations with its neighbors.

The major vulnerability in China's efforts to leverage these tools as a coercive measure would be the risk of international backlash if China's role in fomenting instability were to be revealed. Disclosure of Chinese meddling in the internal affairs of another country could dramatically escalate tensions and impair China's ability to establish a network of client states and broaden its appeal through multilateral institutions.

Offensive Mission 2: Secure Disputed Territory Occupied by U.S. Allies and Partners Through Nonwar Methods

The second offensive mission would be for the PLA to consolidate control over territory claimed by China that is administered by rival countries aligned with the United States. Examples include the Senkaku Islands in the East China Sea and disputed islands and features in the South China Sea. To carry this out, the PLA could leverage nonkinetic methods such as economic coercion, harassment by law enforcement, and information operations to support the Chinese government's efforts to challenge the control exerted by U.S. allies and partners over territory claimed by China. In the context of U.S.-China competition, China would seek not only to reestablish Chinese control over disputed territory but to demonstrate the futility of security guarantees provided by the United States. We assess that such activities would be primarily concentrated along China's periphery and in disputed regions that China claims to be part of its sovereign territory, corresponding to Regions 1 and 2 in our geographic laydown.

We assess there to be one principal task for this mission that is focused on PLA support to civilian authorities in consolidating control over disputed territory (Table 2.7).

This task focuses on PLA support of civilian authority efforts to incrementally increase control over disputed territory occupied by U.S. allies and partners. Beijing has ordered and can continue to order the PLA and associated constabulary and militia units to support civilian authority efforts to administer contested areas. The PLA leverages *gray-zone tactics*, coercive actions short of armed conflict, to convince rivals to simply give up on sovereignty

TABLE 2.7

People's Liberation Army Tasks to Secure Disputed Territory Occupied by U.S. Allies and Partners Through Nonwar Methods (Peacetime Competition Offensive Mission 2)

PLA Task	Chinese Forces	Execution	Coordination: Nonmilitary Assets
Task 1: Support authorities in consolidating control over disputed areas occupied by U.S. allies and partners	• PLA (all services) • PLASSF • CCG • PAFM	• PLA forces carry out patrols, ensure readiness, and coordinate operations with nonmilitary assets for gray-zone operations	• MFA • Propaganda-media • Civilian intelligence and security services, State Council • Provincial governments

disputes amid daunting odds or punishing costs for success.[60] Gray-zone tactics typically involve an incremental approach to changing the facts on the ground, at sea, or in the air in Beijing's favor. Beijing has carried out incremental changes in the status quo, for example, by announcing administrative measures to consolidate China's de facto control of disputed features in the South China and East China seas. It executes these tasks by leveraging not only PLAN but CCG and PAFMM assets to conduct routinized patrols that overwhelm under-resourced opponents.

Using gray-zone tactics at sea is only part of China's approach. In the air domain, for example, the PLAAF is increasingly threatening Taiwan by crossing into its Air Defense Identification Zone (ADIZ) and approaching or crossing the long-standing median line in the Taiwan Strait.[61] These operations are designed, in part, to psychologically pressure Taiwan. Similarly, in October 2021, Beijing passed a new land boundary law that authorized the PLA to take more aggressive action against foreign rivals to defend Chinese sovereignty and territorial integrity.[62] Beijing also directs civilian and PAFM units to aggressively settle and patrol disputed regions, which they reportedly do in such countries as Bhutan and Nepal.[63]

A vulnerability in the PLA's execution of these tasks lies in the risk that military operations to consolidate Chinese control of a border could unintentionally escalate tensions to the point of violence, as happened at the Indian border in 2021.[64] The result could be a serious downturn in China's overall security environment as neighboring countries turn hostile and possibly increase cooperation with the United States. An additional vulnerability is that China's efforts to coerce or intimidate its neighbors are just as likely to harden their neighbor's resolve to challenge China through greater investments in their own warfighting capabilities, seek greater independence from China on diplomatic and political issues, or even secure additional security guarantees from the United States.

Offensive Mission 3: Develop Options to Damage U.S. Overseas Interests

The third likely offensive mission for the PLA in competition with the United States would be to prepare options to militarily damage U.S. interests around the world. The Chinese gov-

---

[60] Lyle J. Morris, Michael J. Mazarr, Jeffrey W. Hornung, Stephanie Pezard, Anika Binnendijk, and Marta Kepe, *Gaining Competitive Advantage in the Gray Zone: Response Options for Coercive Aggression Below the Threshold of Major War*, RAND Corporation, RR-2942-OSD, 2019.

[61] "Thirty Chinese Military Aircraft Enter Taiwan ADIZ," *Focus Taiwan*, May 30, 2022.

[62] Ralph Jennings, "What Does China's New Land Borders Law Mean for Its Neighbors?" *Voice of America*, November 5, 2021.

[63] Robert Barnett, "China is Building Entire Villages in Another Country's Territory," *Foreign Policy*, May 7, 2021.

[64] Jeffrey Gettleman, Emily Schmall, and Hari Kumar, "New India-China Border Clash Shows Simmering Tensions," *New York Times*, September 24, 2021.

ernment is not known to have directed any such task, but Chinese leaders might direct such a mission if tensions with the United States were to escalate. In peacetime, the main mission for the PLA would be to prepare options for sabotage, cyber strikes, or other operations to threaten adversary overseas assets for use in the event of such escalated tensions. PLA access and critical U.S. interests abroad, developed during the competition phase, could also be leveraged by Chinese leadership to deter horizontal escalation by U.S. forces in the event of a larger crisis. This mission would apply to much of the world outside China and the United States, or Regions 2 and 3 in our geographic laydown.

We assess that this mission has one principal task in competition that is focused on the work of the PLA and its civilian counterparts in preparing the environment for such options to be executed, if directed to do so by senior Chinese leadership (Table 2.8).

Intelligence assets in the PLASSF would likely take the lead in identifying vulnerabilities in bases, facilities, networks, and other infrastructure that could be targeted for sabotage. PLA SOF might assist in identifying vulnerabilities in critical infrastructure and develop options for sabotage. Civilian intelligence services could aid in this work as well by recruiting local agents and carrying out reconnaissance that could enable the disruption of specific U.S. interests. In 2018, for example, China reportedly employed lasers against U.S. military aircraft near a PLA military base in Djibouti.[65]

A potential vulnerability in the PLA's ability to develop such options in peacetime lies in the difficulty of gaining and maintaining access to key networks and infrastructure. Cyber networks for militaries allied with the United States are likely to have tighter security than commercial networks, for example. Similarly, Chinese agents would need to find a way to transport arms and equipment to carry out sabotage on foreign soil, which might not be immediately feasible. Developed countries that are distant from China's shores are the most likely to have border control measures in place that could impede efforts to move military weapons and equipment; countries in which corruption is more prevalent might prove more amenable to the movement of such equipment. Similarly, participation in China's Digital Silk Road could open opportunities for PLA cyber units to infiltrate relevant networks in developing countries. Furthermore, China's lack of foreign basing and limited existing partner relationships could limit the PLA's ability to conduct such activities through a partner force.

TABLE 2.8

People's Liberation Army Tasks to Develop Options to Damage U.S. Overseas Interests (Peacetime Competition Offensive Mission 3)

PLA Task	Chinese Forces	Execution	Coordination with Nonmilitary Assets
Task 1: Prepare options to militarily damage U.S., allied overseas interests	• PLASSF • PLA SOF	• PLA works with civilian intelligence to develop accesses, recruit agents, carry out reconnaissance	• Civilian intelligence

---

[65] Aaron Mehta, "Two U.S. Airmen Injured by Chinese Lasers Near Djibouti, DoD Says," *Defense News*, May 3, 2018.

Offensive Mission 4: Weaken and Undermine U.S. Influence, Access, Alliances, and Partnerships

The fourth peacetime offensive mission for competition with the United States would be for the PLA to weaken and undermine U.S. influence, access, alliances, and partnerships. Unlike the first three offensive missions, which focus on options for physical disruption of U.S. interests, this offensive mission directs the PLA to actively erode U.S. influence and support for U.S. interests among its allies and partners. China is known to be carrying out activities to erode U.S. alliances and partnerships and to challenge U.S. influence throughout much of the world. Specifically, we assess that this mission would apply in the Indo-Pacific and other regions outside China and the United States, in Regions 2 and 3.

Specific to the PLA's role in carrying out this mission, we assess that there are two tasks: erode and undermine U.S. influence abroad in key terrains and erode and undermine its broader global narrative (Table 2.9).

First, through defense diplomacy, the PLA can carry out military diplomatic activities to erode and undermine U.S. access, alliances, and partnerships as a means of complicating existing security arrangements between the United States and other nations, particularly nations along China's periphery. China's government could also condition diplomatic and economic benefits on decisions by host nations to curtail security and diplomatic ties to the United States, which appears to have happened in Beijing's dealings with the Solomon Islands in 2022.[66] The PLASSF could also support civilian-led propaganda and diplomatic efforts to delegitimize U.S. military alliances and partnerships in key countries through its own messaging activities. Beijing frequently denounces the United States for maintaining what it calls

TABLE 2.9

People's Liberation Army Tasks to Weaken and Undermine U.S. Influence, Access, and Alliances and Partnerships (Peacetime Competition Offensive Mission 4)

PLA Task	Chinese Forces	Execution	Coordination with Nonmilitary Assets
Task 1: Erode and undermine U.S. military influence, access, partnerships	• PLA (all services) • PAP	• PLA officials pressure host nations to downgrade U.S. access, influence for Chinese benefits	• MFA • Propaganda-media • UFWD
Task 2: Erode and undermine U.S. global narrative on security topics	• PLASSF	• PLA specialists support civilian propaganda, messaging	• MFA • Propaganda-media • UFWD

---

[66] Edward Wong, "Solomon Islands Suspends Visits by Foreign Military Ships, Raising Concerns in U.S.," *New York Times*, April 30, 2022.

a "Cold War mentality" that aims to "contain" China in "zero-sum" competition.[67] China's government often attempts to persuade countries that political, economic, and security cooperation with China will better ensure their interests than alignment with the United States.[68]

The second task entails undermining the U.S. global narrative. For this task, Beijing could instruct the PLA to engage in military demonstrations and conduct media warfare, psychological operations, and legal warfare activities to discredit U.S. political and military power. The PLASSF could aid in cyber operations in support of the civilian-led MFA and UFWD, and in support of propaganda-media outlets engaged in influence operations.

A potential vulnerability in the PLA's execution of both tasks is that countries could reject China's overtures, especially if China appeared to overreach with influence-peddling activities within their sovereign territory. Beijing has often reacted to such rejection with anger, creating potential opportunities for the United States and its allies to leverage diplomatic openings with countries subject to Chinese backlash. In some cases, China has imposed coercive penalties to signal its frustration and displeasure with such acts. The result has often been a weakening of Chinese influence and partnerships. Examples can be seen in the deterioration of China's relationship with South Korea following China's economic coercion in response to South Korea's deployment of a U.S. theater missile defense system.[69]

Overview of the People's Liberation Army's Vulnerabilities in Peacetime Competition

This chapter has provided an analysis of potential PLA missions to support China's competitive strategy against the United States. Our list of PLA missions and tasks provides a framework through which U.S. military planners can understand the wide variety of activities that China's military could attempt in competition with the United States and that China is already pursuing in many parts of the world. More importantly, our analysis derives various hypothesized vulnerabilities in the PLA's ability to successfully execute these missions in pursuit of the China Dream. Table 2.10 summarizes these assessed PLA vulnerabilities that are associated with each mission.

These vulnerabilities provide a sense of the difficulties and potential pressure points that the PLA is likely to face in accomplishing its peacetime competition objectives and the challenges that CCP decisionmakers face in leveraging the military instrument of power to achieve their objectives short of war. Broadly, these peacetime competition vulnerabilities fall into five main categories:

---

[67] Jamey Keaten, "China's Xi Rejects 'Cold War Mentality,' Pushes Cooperation," Associated Press, January 17, 2022.

[68] Keaten, 2022.

[69] Ethan Meick and Nargiza Salidjanova, *China's Response to U.S.-South Korea Missile Defense System Deployment and Its Implications*, U.S. China Economic and Security Review Commission, July 2017.

TABLE 2.10

Peacetime Competition People's Liberation Army Missions and Potential Vulnerabilities

PLA Missions	Potential Vulnerabilities
Defensive Mission 1: Deter and defeat externally backed threats to CCP, basic security, and socialist system	• Politicization of the PLA as a tool for domestic power • Accelerated domestic unrest and dissatisfaction with the CCP for using the PLA to suppress domestic protests • Potential reputational blowback that damages market access and influence abroad
Defensive Mission 2: Defend China's territory, sovereignty, and national unity from U.S.-backed threats	• Concerns over risk of unintended escalation stymie decisionmaking • Potential reputational backlash and aggravated threat perceptions from aggressive measures to protect Chinese sovereignty claims • Unknown adequacy of PLA forces and execution of military operations
Defensive Mission 3: Defend Chinese overseas interests from U.S.-backed threats	• Inadequate power projection capabilities • Limited ability and experience assisting partner states with security needs and potential reputational damage from failure to do so • Aggravated threat perceptions in response to Chinese coercion • Domestic sensitivity to PLA casualties
Defensive Mission 4: Defend China's influence, access, partnerships, and narrative from U.S. subversion attempts	• Limited impact of military diplomacy and information operations on broader efforts to promote to political, economic relationships • Limited experience working with foreign partners, and limited appeal compared with U.S. security partnerships
Offensive Mission 1: Undermine and threaten governments, basic security, and social systems of U.S. and its allies	• Disclosure of Chinese government involvement could damage China's reputation and influence
Offensive Mission 2: Support threats to the territory and sovereignty of U.S. allies	• Aggressive measures to consolidate control could create instability on China's borders • Aggressive measures could harden adversary resolve
Offensive Mission 3: Support threats to overseas interests of the United States and its allies	• Difficulty in accessing U.S., allied networks and facilities • Disclosure of efforts to develop options could fuel tensions, damage China's reputation • Limited overseas posture and partner relationships
Offensive Mission 4: Undermine U.S. influence, access, alliances, partnerships, and narrative	• Chinese efforts to undermine alliances could backfire, weakening China's reputation and influence

- Fears of Chinese domestic instability: These vulnerabilities arise from the potential for instability in China that could arise from the PLA's execution of tasks. For peacetime competition, they consist of the potential for domestic backlash to PLA participation in domestic repression, persistent questions about the loyalty of the armed forces and the potential for defiance of orders or the formation of factions in a domestic crisis, and potential popular backlash over PLA casualties abroad in operations to defend Chinese interests. These vulnerabilities stem primarily from defensive missions in peacetime competition.

- Escalation risk: These vulnerabilities consist of potential unwanted expansion of conflict or damage to China's economic prospects. In peacetime competition, they include the potential for serious miscalculations in offensive and defensive missions along China's borders that could create instability or generate escalation into conflict.

- Reputational risk: These vulnerabilities arise from the potential for action or the lack of action taken by the PLA to damage China's reputation, influence, and appeal as a partner. In peacetime competition, they include concerns about the potential disclosure of Chinese involvement in offensive efforts to degrade the legitimacy, overseas interests, or influence of the United States and its partner nations and the potential for such coercion to harden adversary resolve and diminish the desire of potential partner nations to cooperate with China. These vulnerabilities are the most extensive across our analysis of the PLA's roles in peacetime competition and apply to most, if not all, of the PLA's offensive and defensive missions.

- Limited ability to support partners: These vulnerabilities consist of potential failures in PLA efforts to aid partner forces abroad. In peacetime competition, this includes the PLA's limited familiarity with foreign cultures, limited experience operating in foreign languages, and limited experience in helping partners address internal threats through security cooperation. Yet another constraint is the PLA's limited ability to operate through partners to conduct military operations that serve Chinese interests. These vulnerabilities primarily affect China's efforts to defend its own overseas interests and influence or to degrade the interests and influence of the United States. and its partners.

- Limited ability to project power: These vulnerabilities arise from the potential for actions taken by the PLA to fail in execution as a result of a limited ability to conduct military operations far from the Chinese mainland. In peacetime competition, this includes concerns about the PLA's logistical ability to enable major operations outside China's immediate periphery, its lack of overseas bases, and its limited prior overseas experience conducting major military operations. These factors affect the PLA's ability to defend against threats to China's territorial sovereignty and overseas interests or degrade the overseas interests of the United States and its partner nations.

We reiterate that these vulnerabilities represent analytic hypotheses that are worthy of further research and validation. However, they do offer analytically informed baseline assessments intended to promote further thinking on ways to disrupt and counter Chinese peacetime strategies that might threaten U.S. interests.

We will explore the implications of these vulnerabilities to potential U.S. efforts to disrupt the Chinese military in Chapter 5. In Chapter 3, we turn to the PLA's missions and tasks in a potential low-intensity war with the United States.

A Scenario for U.S.-China Low-Intensity Conflict

In this chapter, we analyze potential PLA missions, tasks, and vulnerabilities in a hypothetical U.S.-China low-intensity conflict. We choose to focus on a low-intensity conflict scenario for two reasons. First, there already exists a substantial body of research and analysis on the potential for large-scale, high-intensity war between the United States and China, typically centered on a Taiwan contingency.[1] Second, low-intensity conflict between China and the United States remains a poorly understood yet distinct possibility. Some analysts have pointed to hybrid, irregular, and other variants of low-intensity war as a more likely form of U.S.-China conflict than large-scale conventional war because of the overwhelming costs that such a conflict would impose on them.[2] However, to date, there has been little analysis on this topic.

To be clear, there is no publicly available information to suggest that China is contemplating a limited war with the United States in the manner described in the subsequent sections. However, the possibility that U.S.-China relations could deteriorate into hostility cannot be fully discounted. Should such a situation unfold, Beijing could face strikingly powerful incentives to pursue more-aggressive polices that are at odds with its traditional behavior.

A low-intensity conflict could take many forms, as the United States and Soviet Union experienced during the Cold War. In some cases, the United States could find itself supporting a partner government against Chinese-backed nonstate actors—perhaps in areas more distant from China, such as Latin America or the Middle East. The PLA's limited power projection capability would make large-scale Chinese military intervention in those areas unlikely, but arms sales and support to nonstate actors could aim to exhaust U.S. military resources in a protracted conflict. The reverse is also possible. Low-intensity conflict could take the form of U.S. support to nonstate actors that are engaged in hostilities against a Chinese-backed government or vice versa, perhaps in countries along China's periphery.

---

[1] Eric Heginbotham, Michael Nixon, Forrest Morgan, Jacob Heim, Jeff Hagan, Sheng Li, Jeffrey Engstrom, Martin Libicki, Paul DeLuca, David Shlapak, David Frelinger, Burgess Laird, Kyle Brady, and Lyle Morris, *The U.S. China Military Scorecard: Forces, Geography, and the Evolving Balance of Power 1996–2017*, RAND Corporation, RR-392-AF, 2015.

[2] Efron, Klein, and Cohen, 2020.

This support could take a form similar to that of U.S. support to Mujahedeen fighters against the Soviet Union in 1980s Afghanistan. In yet other cases, both sides could find themselves backing rival states or nonstate groups within a nation. Low-intensity conflict could also include a variety of hybrid or irregular warfare methods, including cyberattacks, information warfare, and gray-zone activities that involve paramilitary forces. China already uses some of these methods in peacetime. The difference in a scenario of low-intensity conflict would be the far more extensive use of such tactics by Chinese forces, in addition to more aggressive and potentially lethal operations that could risk greater escalation of conflict with the United States.

With the hypothetical scenario presented in this chapter, we aim to stimulate thinking about such a scenario. We also aim to provide an aid for analysts and defense planners who are preparing for the full variety of potential hostile actions involving the PLA, not just large-scale combat operations. Although we lay out key assumptions to frame this analysis, our main purpose is not to predict the outcome of such a scenario or narrate how it might unfold but to describe the potential set of PLA missions and tasks under such conditions and what they might mean for U.S. efforts to disrupt the PLA in such a scenario.

The chapter is organized in the following manner. First, we describe how the current peacetime competition between the U.S. and China could transition into a low-intensity war. To do this, we posit a *transition phase* in the U.S.-China relationship during which the current situation would escalate into an unstable, crisis-filled environment with high potential for conflict. We then briefly describe the context in which a low-intensity conflict between China and the United States could occur, focusing on the potential for each side to indirectly attack the other's interests using limited violence. In the bulk of the chapter, we develop our list of the specific tasks that the PLA would likely be directed to carry out in such a war, along with associated potential PLA vulnerabilities.

Transition from Peacetime to Conflict

The current U.S.-China relationship features a great deal of tension, but, by all accounts, the risk of war remains low.[3] The two countries do not yet regard each other as bitter enemies in the way that the United States and the Soviet Union did during the Cold War, and there is little incentive for either side to pursue policies that directly threaten the other. Our analysis of the PLA's potential behavior in a low-intensity conflict cannot begin with the status quo but requires assumptions regarding a change in the political-strategic situation that incentivizes Beijing to direct more-aggressive actions by the PLA.

History provides evidence of distinct patterns in interstate behavior that tend to precede the onset of hostilities. Key trends that historically accompany the momentum to conflict include an intensification of mutual threat perceptions, arms racing behavior, coalition-

---

[3] Dobbins et al., 2017.

building activity aimed at the other state, and the occurrence of a series of militarized crises.[4] For the purposes of this analysis, we assume a similar transformation in the current U.S.-China peacetime relationship to an unstable, crisis-filled situation featuring a high risk of escalation. We will call this hypothetical situation a *transition phase*, which we define as an unstable bilateral relationship featuring acute perceptions of mutual threat and political momentum toward conflict. The transition phase represents a period of time between peacetime competition and a hypothetical state of conflict.

In such a transition phase, there is great potential for a sequence of interrelated militarized crises to occur between the two rivals. Militarized crises can be both a symptom and an accelerant of the unstable relationship.[5] How Chinese decisionmakers respond to any crisis will depend on the circumstances of that crisis. There might be a possibility of restoring stability in cases in which mutual threat perceptions have not yet become acute and in which momentum toward war is not yet present. In other cases, however, Chinese decisionmakers might conclude that violence is inevitable and accordingly exploit a crisis to better position Chinese forces to prevail in the anticipated conflict.

Given the turbulent and unstable nature of such a transition, demarcating when the onset of a low-intensity, undeclared "war" begins is not easy. One way to do so is to assess the stated policy positions of the contending governments. The onset of a period of low-intensity conflict could begin when the two governments designate each other as a threat to survival and explicitly direct their armed forces to carry out operations against the rival power. The issuance of National Security Directive 68 by President Harry Truman in 1950, which directed U.S. efforts to contain the Soviet Union, provides a clear example of such a decision point. Similarly, directives from Chairman Mao to regard the Soviet Union as the principal threat to Chinese survival in the 1960s provides a similar example from China's history.[6]

It is important to stress how such a situation differs from the situation in 2023. Both the U.S. and Chinese governments have described each other as competitors and as carrying some level of threat to each other's specific interests, but neither has identified the other as a direct threat to the nation's basic security, survival, or most-vital interests. The two governments do not regard war with the other as likely or desirable. On the contrary, both governments have expressed the desire to avoid war and maintain cooperative relations even as they disagree profoundly on specific issues, such as Taiwan and the South China Sea.[7] Our scenario begins with the assumption that the U.S.-China relationship has already deteriorated

---

[4] Timothy R. Heath and Matthew Lane, *Science Based Scenario Design: A Proposed Method to Support Political-Strategic Analysis*, RAND Corporation, RR-2833-OSD, 2019.

[5] Michael Brecher, "Crisis, Conflict, War: The State of the Discipline," *International Political Science Review*, Vol. 17, No. 2, April 1996.

[6] John Gaddis, *The Cold War: A New History*, Penguin Books, 2005.

[7] Hoo Tiang Boon, "Xi-Biden Summit: Finding the Contours of Responsible Competition," *Straits Times*, November 18, 2021; "Xiplomacy: Xi's Call for China-U.S. Cooperation on Global Issues," Xinhua, November 18, 2021.

from one of relative stability into something far more unstable and dangerous. However, we emphasize this is an assumption, not a prediction.

U.S.-China Low-Intensity Conflict: Key Assumptions

For the purposes of our analysis of a hypothetical low-intensity U.S.-China conflict, we assume that this transition phase in U.S.-China relations has already passed and the situation has escalated into one of hostilities between the two countries that remains short of outright conventional war. Each side not only perceives the other as its primary adversary in world affairs but actively seeks to undermine the other where possible around the world. The conflict is therefore global albeit indirect. Many aspects of China's policy would have changed once the two sides entered a state of declared or undeclared low-intensity conflict. For example, China would likely have adopted a more activist foreign policy to actively support adversaries of the United States in a move reminiscent of how involved China became in international politics during the Cold War. Ideologically, China might have adopted a more nationalist or anti-U.S. ideology to rally domestic and international support. Articulating some ideology could help China recruit allies and partners and aid its messaging efforts.

Similar to the U.S. experience in the Cold War, a low-intensity conflict between China and the United States would likely involve many third parties. Symptomatic of the hostile state of relations, we assume that both nations have dramatically increased arms buildups aimed primarily at the other's interests abroad. Both have also likely stepped up efforts to expand their coalitions of security partners and equipped them accordingly. We assume that the governments of the two countries face strong popular support within their own countries for hostile action against the rival country and little support for conciliatory policies. The bilateral relationship has accordingly ceased or curtailed much of their international cooperation.

In this situation, the political leaders of each country have already designated the other country as a major threat to the nation's well-being and authorized military hostilities against the other. However, because of fears of escalation, both sides restrict military action to indirect or proxy-led violence. Moreover, both sides have judged that such low-intensity violence will not automatically prompt the other to escalate the conflict to conventional or nuclear war. For the purposes of structuring the analysis, we posit that the conflict begins at least after the year 2030. However, we emphasize this is merely an assumption to help frame our analysis, not a prediction.

Throughout the transition to hostilities, we assume that Chinese military capabilities have continued to advance. The PLA's cyber and long-range missile capabilities would have expanded significantly at this stage, and Chinese stealth bomber and long-range transport projects would have come to full fruition. The size of the PLAN's carrier force and long-range transport fleet would have grown significantly, and current deficiencies in PLA SOF, and the PLA's broader global communications and command, control, communications, computers, ISR capabilities would have been addressed. On the diplomatic front, we assume that

China's international influence has continued to grow, especially along the rim of the Indian Ocean, in Africa, in Eastern Europe, and in some parts of Latin America. In some cases, this influence has resulted in greater military cooperation and even military access. Finally, we assume that the PLA would be under orders from political authorities in Beijing to maintain close coordination with diplomatic and economic efforts, employ low-cost asymmetric means where possible, seize and maintain the moral and political high ground, and control escalation. Indirect and proxy war is therefore Beijing's preferred approach.

It is worth underscoring how much this scenario would represent a departure from recent Chinese military and diplomatic behavior. Although China does cultivate and exploit economic dependencies, it has eschewed any formal military commitments since the end of the Cold War.[8] Moreover, at least since the end of the Cold War, the Chinese have not made any serious, large-scale attempts to destabilize sitting regimes.[9]

China's Policy Aims in a Limited Conflict Scenario

In such a scenario, Beijing has already assessed that the defeat of U.S. power has become a necessary condition for achieving the China Dream. After all, Washington's ability to deny Beijing's realization of an end state on which the CCP has staked its legitimacy offers the most plausible reason for China to risk war. Therefore, in this scenario, Chinese leaders have judged that they must break U.S. power in their pursuit of the China Dream. This section expands on similar analysis in a previous report about scenarios of U.S.-China systemic conflict.[10]

In this scenario, Beijing has thus designated the defeat of U.S. willingness and ability to forestall China's realization of its national revitalization goals as a top strategic imperative. Beijing's desired end state accepts the continuation of the United States as a nation but one in a much diminished and weakened condition. In effect, China's end state envisions its ascent to a position of global preeminence and the concomitant downgrading of the status of the United States to a primarily regional power in the Americas. A U.S. presence in the rest of the world would unavoidably continue but only on terms acceptable to China. At the same time, Chinese leaders in this scenario would aim to avoid a great-power war, the escalation of which could prove impossible to control and which would carry intolerably high risks of nuclear exchange. Beijing might even seek to sustain a trading relationship and some level of stable ties. Somewhat similar to Chinese descriptions of an ideal "new type of major power

---

[8] Eva Dou, "What Is—and Isn't—in the Joint Statement from Putin and Xi," *Washington Post*, February 4, 2022.

[9] Timothy R. Heath, Christian Curriden, Bryan Frederick, Nathan Chandler, and Jennifer Kavanagh, *China's Military Interventions: Patterns, Drivers, and Signposts*, RAND Corporation, RR-A444-4, 2021, pp. 67–68.

[10] Heath, Gunness, and Finazzo.

relationship," the ideal end state for China in the event of a low-intensity conflict with the United States would be a return to peace on terms of nominal equality with de facto U.S. deference to China as the new global leading power.[11] However, this is not the only possibility. The acrimony generated by incessant conflict, even indirect conflict, could also be enough to seriously disrupt ties to an extent that large-scale war becomes the only outcome.

We assess that China's goals for Sino-American relations in such a scenario would consist of the following objectives:

1. High intensity major war with the United States is avoided.
2. The United States no longer contests China's position as global leader.
3. The United States refrains from threatening China's interests.
4. The United States no longer actively contests Chinese primacy across Eurasia, the Middle East, and Africa.
5. U.S. primacy has been reduced to the Americas.
6. Cooperation and resolution of differences with the United States are carried out on terms acceptable to China.[12]

China's Military Strategy in a Low-Intensity Conflict

In a low-intensity conflict, the PLA would play a leading role in China's overall national strategy. Many aspects of Chinese foreign policy likely would have changed to accommodate the onset of hostilities. For example, in such a situation, China might be more willing to assist client states with more-robust military assistance. Although we acknowledge the likelihood that many aspects of China's policies would have experienced dramatic changes in the event of war, we focus on the key missions and tasks that the PLA might be expected to assume, drawing from our framework of core Chinese national interests that was developed in Chapter 2.

China's Military Strategic Missions

The potential set of missions assigned to the PLA in a low-intensity conflict scenario builds on the four broad sets of missions provided in the analysis of peacetime competition in Chapter 2 and are adapted from prior RAND research to facilitate our more granular analysis of PLA tasks and vulnerabilities later in this chapter (Table 3.1).[13] These missions are similarly paired between defensive and offensive versions of broader military objectives to support

---

[11] Cheng Li and Lucy Xu, "Chinese Enthusiasm and American Cynicism over the 'New Type of Great Power Relations,'" Brookings Institution, December 4, 2014.

[12] For a much more in-depth examination of these goals, see Chapter 2 and Heath, Grossman, and Clark, 2019, p. xv.

[13] See Table 6.4 in Heath, Gunness, and Finazzo, 2022, p. 94.

TABLE 3.1

People's Liberation Army Strategic Missions in a Low-Intensity Conflict Scenario

Core Interests	Defensive Missions	Offensive Mission
Political and social stability	Defensive Mission 1: Deter and defeat externally backed threats to CCP, basic security, and socialist system	Offensive Mission 1: Undermine and threaten government, basic security, and social system of U.S. and allies
Basic security, national sovereignty, territorial integrity	Defensive Mission 2: Deter and defeat U.S.-backed threats to China's territory, sovereignty, and national unity	Offensive Mission 2: Threaten territory and sovereignty of U.S. allies and partners
Overseas interests	Defensive Mission 3: Deter and defeat externally backed threats to Chinese overseas interests	Offensive Mission 3: Threaten key overseas interests of U.S., allies
International influence, partnerships, narrative	Defensive Mission 4: Defend China's influence, access, partnerships, and narrative from subversion from external threats	Offensive Mission 4: Undermine U.S. influence, alliances and partnerships, access, and narrative

SOURCES: Features information from Heath, Grossman, and Clark, 2021; and Heath, Gunness, and Finazzo, 2022.

vital national interests. A key difference during low-intensity conflict lies in the more aggressive and hostile nature of such military missions. This aggression reflects presumed directives from Chinese political leadership to weaken and discredit U.S. power globally as part of a struggle for supremacy. It also assumes that Chinese leadership has authorized the PLA to indirectly engage U.S. forces when the risk of escalation appears manageable. This list of missions is not exhaustive, but it represents a broad framework that helps guide our analysis of potential PLA vulnerabilities in such a scenario.

The second column in Table 3.1 lists the defensive missions that the PLA might be expected to undertake in a U.S.-China low-intensity conflict. Defensive Mission 1 concerns efforts to deter and defeat threats to CCP rule, basic security, and Chinese society. Defensive Mission 2 calls on the PLA to deter and defeat threats to Chinese sovereignty and territory. Defensive Mission 3 directs the PLA to deter and defeat threats to Chinese citizens and their assets abroad and threats to the core interests of key client states. In Defensive Mission 4, Beijing directs the PLA to defeat threats to Chinese influence, access, partnerships, and China's grip on the global narrative.

The third column lists potential offensive missions that the PLA might be directed to undertake against U.S. interests. Offensive Mission 1 directs the PLA to undermine and threaten the legitimacy of rival states, potentially including the United States and its key allies and partners. Offensive Mission 2 calls on the PLA to secure control of contested territory and sovereignty. Offensive Mission 3 directs the PLA to threaten key overseas interests that belong to the United States and its allies. In Offensive Mission 4, Beijing directs the PLA to aggressively undermine U.S. influence, access, alliances, partnerships, and narratives. For both the offensive and defensive missions, Chinese leaders would insist on careful management of escalation to avoid instigating a large-scale conventional war or worse.

People's Liberation Army Defensive Missions in a Low-Intensity Conflict

To translate these broad missions into more-discrete military activities, we have listed potential PLA tasks to support low-intensity conflict missions globally. For each proposed mission and task, we assess possible PLA military forces that could be involved and articulate how each task might be executed. We also describe key nonmilitary Chinese assets that could support the PLA. Similarly, we hypothesize possible vulnerabilities for each task.

Defensive Mission 1: Deter and Defeat Externally Backed Threats to Chinese Communist Party, Basic Security, and Socialist System

In a low-intensity conflict with the United States, a basic PLA defensive responsibility would be to ensure the survival of the CCP regime and the Chinese nation. Although a large-scale land invasion is not a threat, Chinese writers have noted the vulnerability of vital civilian and military infrastructure within China.[14] The PLA has taken precautions against aerial bombing, cyberattacks, and sabotage.[15] These activities would focus on the Chinese homeland, which is Region 1 in our geographic laydown.

We assess that there are three basic tasks for the PLA associated with this defensive mission in a low-intensity conflict: deterring and responding to physical threats to the Chinese mainland, managing potential threats to CCP legitimacy in Han-dominant and ethnic-minority regions, and deterring adversary efforts to delegitimize the CCP through information operations against the Chinese mainland. These tasks are summarized in Table 3.2.

Should a low-intensity conflict erupt, China's fears over the potential for attacks against its homeland are likely to increase, and the PLA would be given a prominent role in defending critical military, economic, and government personnel and infrastructure from cyber, SOF, or air attack as a first task. The PAP likely would play a key role in these infrastructure and facilities defense missions, PLAAF air defense units would increase their preparations for anti-air campaigns, and PLASSF forces would step up cybersecurity measures.[16] The PLASSF would likely be responsible for protecting China's military and civilian infrastructure in space, and both the PLASSF and PLARF would be assigned the task of prepar-

---

[14] Yu Jin, ed., *The Science of Second Artillery Operations* [第二炮兵战役学], People's Liberation Army Press, trans. by Gregory Kulacki, September 19, 2014, pp. 294–296.

[15] Huang Linhao [黄林昊], "Chinese Representative Calls for the Creation of a Digital Database to Prevent the Cross-Border Flow of Terrorists [中国代表呼吁尽快建立数据库遏制恐怖分子跨国流动]," *People's Daily* [人民日报], June 17, 2015; Liu Wei [刘伟], "Building a City's Anti-Air Efforts into a Modern 'Iron Fortress,'" [打造现代城市防空的" 铜墙铁壁"], *China Defense* [中国国防报], May 15, 2019; State Council Information Office, "Regulations for the Protection of Critical Information Infrastructure [关键信息基础设施安全保护条例]," July 30, 2021.

[16] Joel Wuthnow, *China's Other Army: The People's Armed Police in an Era of Reform*, National Defense University Press, April 16, 2019, p. 2.

TABLE 3.2

People's Liberation Army Tasks to Deter and Defeat Externally Backed Threats to the Chinese Communist Party, Basic Security, and Socialist System (Low-Intensity Conflict Defensive Mission 1)

Tasks	Chinese Forces	Execution	Coordination with Nonmilitary Assets
Task 1: Deter externally backed conventional, space, cyber, and nuclear strikes	• PAP • PLA (all services)	• PLA cyber units support domestic law enforcement to protect cyber infrastructure • PLA intelligence helps monitor foreign threats to space, domestic infrastructure • PAP patrols and guards facilities; • PLARF carries out deterrence missions	• Civilian intelligence and security services • Militia • MFA • Propaganda-media • CAC
Task 2: Control threats to CCP rule in Han-dominant and ethnic-minority regions	• PAP • PLAGF • PAFM	• PAP, PLA forces augment law enforcement in monitoring and suppressing popular protests, demonstrations, and other potential externally backed domestic challenges to CCP rule • PAP, PLA forces capture any foreign agents fomenting unrest	• Civilian intelligence and security services • UFWD • CAC
Task 3: Deter and defeat enemy efforts to undermine CCP rule through information operations	• PLASSF • Joint Staff Department's Information and Communications Bureau	• PLASSF carries out reconnaissance of enemy cyber forces, operations to counter U.S.-disinformation and other information operations	• Propaganda-media • Civilian intelligence and security services • CAC

ing retaliatory counter–space attacks to deter external threats against space infrastructure as part of a low-intensity war. PLA units likely would work closely with local governments and the Ministry of Public Security.

Of course, the most devastating possible outcome of any low- or high-intensity conflict with the United States would be a miscalculation that drives either side to escalate to nuclear strikes. The PLARF would be tasked with ensuring the readiness of a credible nuclear counterattack capability.[17] China is also likely to benefit from ongoing efforts to strengthen its strategic nuclear triad by building a fleet of nuclear-capable bombers and submarines.[18]

A second task for the PLA would be to guard against uprisings in either Han-dominated or ethnic-minority regions. One of China's greatest fears is the emergence of a foreign-backed color revolution or popular uprising within its own territory. Local governments and the Ministry of Public Security would have the primary responsibility of monitoring the domestic population and heading off any major antigovernment movement, but the PLA is seen as an important last-resort fail-safe should law enforcement fail to protect the party from its people.[19] PAP mobile detachments deployed throughout the country would likely support local law enforcement as needed to put down protests, protect government buildings, respond to disasters, and address other emergencies.[20] The PLA would potentially be tasked with helping identify foreign agents behind any opposition movement during any low-intensity conflict with the United States, even if such a conflict were to occur far from China's borders. Chinese leaders have already shown concern over the potential for foreign meddling in local protest movements that challenge Chinese rule.[21]

A third task would be for the PLA to respond to and deter attacks or subversion by foreign agents in the information domain, especially in cyberspace. This task involves protecting key infrastructure from cyberattacks by U.S. forces and rapidly controlling or diffusing any viral online movements or narratives that the CCP finds dangerous.[22] Although the responsibility for controlling cyberspace predominantly falls to such civilian agencies as the CAC and Ministry of Public Security, the PLASSF and the Information Support Base of the PLA Joint Staff Department's Information and Communications Bureau might play a role, although the relationships between these organizations remain murky.[23] In the event of a low-intensity conflict, greater responsibility for domestic information security might be devolved onto the PLA. The CCP believes that a failure to control information domestically could pose an exis-

[17] Anthony H. Cordesman and Joseph Kendall, *Chinese Strategy and Military Modernization in 2016*, Center for Strategic and International Studies, 2016.

[18] Mike Yeo and Robert Burns, "Pentagon Warns of China's Progress Toward Nuclear Triad," *Military Times*, November 4, 2021.

[19] Philip C. Saunders and Joel Wuthnow, "Large and In Charge: Civil-Military Relations Under Xi Jinping," in Philip C. Saunders, Arthur S. Ding, Andrew Scobell, Andrew N. D. Yang, and Joel Wuthnow, eds. *Chairman Xi Remakes the PLA: Assessing Chinese Military Reforms*, National Defense University Press, 2019

[20] Wuthnow, 2019.

[21] Andrew Higgins, "China's Theory for Hong Kong Protests: Secret American Meddling," *New York Times*, August 8, 2019.

[22] Ryan Fedasiuk, "Buying Silence: The Price of Internet Censorship in China," *China Brief*, Vol. 21, No. 1, January 12, 2021.

[23] Costello and McReynolds, 2019, pp. 53–54.

tential threat to its rule and will likely use all the tools at its disposal, including the PLA, to prevent the United States or any other foreign power from exploiting this vulnerability.[24]

These tasks carry two fundamental vulnerabilities for the CCP. Similar to all major economic powers, China relies on a large number of interdependent, soft civilian infrastructure targets that are difficult to defend and that could cause immense hardship if destroyed. Although military infrastructure is generally somewhat easier to defend, it also can be vulnerable to cyber threats, ground raids, or air attacks. The result could be damage to the nation's economic prospects and a potential increase in social instability because of civilian casualties and the dislocation caused by military strikes.

Another potential vulnerability in China's execution of its homeland defense tasks is the burden that military security measures might place on economic activity and social stability. The Chinese government expends immense resources to monitor and control its own population and is constantly vigilant against opposition movements, whether they originate at home or abroad.[25] Citizens could chafe at the inconveniences, high cost, and repressiveness of elevated military security measures. The heightened security posture could also prove detrimental to broader economic growth through added costs of security measures, adverse impacts on business climate, and added systemic risk for international trade and finance.

Defensive Mission 2: Deter and Defeat Externally Backed Threats to China's Territory, Sovereignty, and National Unity

One of the PLA's fundamental missions in a low-intensity conflict would still be the physical defense of Chinese borders and territorial sovereignty from externally backed threats. For the purposes of this scenario, we assume that Taiwan's status has not yet been resolved—neither China nor Taiwan prove willing to unify peacefully and China is not yet ready to risk high-intensity war to achieve unification. Tasks to support this mission would center on the Chinese homeland, Region 1 in our geographic laydown.

We assess that the PLA would be called on to perform three primary tasks to defend against threats to China's territorial sovereignty during a broader low-intensity conflict with the United States. These consist of efforts to defend against maritime and ground incursions into border areas, efforts to control potential separatist threats in western provinces, and efforts to deter Taiwan from asserting its independence during a low-intensity conflict through coercive measures. These tasks are summarized in Table 3.3.

Deterrence and defeat of any externally backed threats to Chinese territory could include operations and activities on land and at sea, the first task for the PLA under this defensive mission. China has occasionally demonstrated its willingness to use limited lethal force against rival border disputants, such as the clash between local border troops and Indian

---

[24] Costello and McReynolds, 2019, p. 48.

[25] Josh Chin, "China Spends More on Domestic Security as Xi's Powers Grow," *Wall Street Journal*, March 6, 2018.

TABLE 3.3

People's Liberation Army Tasks to Deter and Defeat Externally Backed Threats to China's Territory, Sovereignty, and National Unity (Low-Intensity Conflict Defensive Mission 2)

Tasks	Chinese Forces	Execution	Coordination with Nonmilitary Assets
Task 1: Deter and defeat incursions into land and maritime border areas by externally backed adversaries	• PLA (all services) • PLASSF • CCG • Militia	• Joint forces carry out combat operations to drive any forces that invade Chinese territory out while controlling escalation	• Civilian intelligence and security services • UFWD • MFA • State Council • Provincial governments
Task 2: Defeat separatist threats in western provinces	• PAP • PLASSF • PLAGF	• PAP augments law enforcement in suppressing large-scale riots, carrying out counterterror operations, and patrolling minority regions • PLA supports security as necessary and helps locate and neutralize foreign agents	• Civilian intelligence and security services • UFWD • MFA
Task 3: Defend and defeat Taiwan separatist movements	• PLA (all services) • CCG • Militia	• PLA joint force carries out deterrence operations; conducts coercive gray-zone actions to prevent Taiwan independence	• Civilian intelligence and security services • UFWD, State Council • TAO

troops in 2020.[26] Perhaps the area in which the PLA has been most frequently called on to defend Chinese territorial claims has been the South China Sea and other disputed waters. Here, the PAFMM, which operates under civil and military authority, is Beijing's first line of defense and offense. These are civilian vessels that are sometimes augmented with military communication or navigation gear and whose crews receive limited military training. They can be called on to swarm sensitive areas by the hundreds, chasing away or harassing the vessels of rival claimants.[27] In a low-intensity conflict scenario, the militia could also be called on to either provide surveillance or more aggressively harass U.S., allied, and partner ships, perhaps engaging with limited violence as a provocative measure and inviting opportunities to exploit any military response by external actors against civilian vessels in the informa-

---

[26] "India-China Clash: 20 Indian Troops Killed in Ladakh Fighting," BBC News, June 16, 2020.

[27] Luo Shuxian and Jonathan G. Panter, "China's Maritime Militia and Fishing Fleets," *Military Review*, January–February 2021, pp. 16–17.

tion environment.[28] Civilian intelligence, propaganda-media organizations, the MFA, and the UFWD would likely play prominent roles in such tasks.

Second, the PLA would likely play key roles in preparing for and responding to any potential separatist violence in China's ethnic-minority regions. Because of China's tendency to conflate domestic opposition with foreign infiltration, an even greater degree of militarization of domestic security is likely in the event of a low-intensity conflict with the United States.[29] The PLAGF and, especially, PAP could be called on to prepare for and respond to large-scale separatist uprisings in restive border regions or to assist civilian law enforcement agencies in surveilling and incarcerating members of ethnic minorities with a history of separatism.[30] Although civilian law enforcement agencies (mostly from the Ministry of Public Security and its local organs) have primary responsibility for the sprawling surveillance and detention complex in Xinjiang, PAP units would likely provide extra manpower and firepower as needed if any separatist violence were to overwhelm local police.[31] The PAP also has several specialized counterterror special operations units that could be used against any nonstate actors that Beijing regards as a threat.[32]

In a broader low-intensity conflict, CCP leadership might choose to refrain from invading Taiwan because of fears of escalation into direct conflict with the United States. But, as a third task, the PLA would likely carry out gray-zone operations to coerce and punish Taiwan to disincentivize any efforts by Taiwan's leadership to take advantage of the broader conflict to assert greater independence. Options could include maritime quarantines and other naval actions aimed at Taiwanese shipping. PLA forces could also seize outlying Taiwanese-held islands. The goal of such intimidation tactics would be to wear down Taiwan's leadership with more-aggressive rules of engagement. The PLA would coordinate these efforts with civilian authorities, including the TAO, the UFWD, and civilian security and intelligence services.

The PLA faces several potential vulnerabilities in its execution of these missions. One is the limited capability and prior experience of PLA forces in executing large-scale military operations, including major operations to secure a border area or widespread coercive actions against Taiwan short of an outright invasion. These vulnerabilities could become particularly acute in the event that such a conflict were to become protracted. Furthermore, any PLA coercive action against Taiwan or its leadership could create a public backlash in Taiwan, further erode an already low base of support for unification, and possibly harden the resolve

---

[28] Luo Shuxian and Panter, 2021, p. 17.

[29] Matthew Brooker, "'Red Roulette' Uncovers Covert Hands in Hong Kong," *Bloomberg*, October 3, 2021.

[30] Wuthnow, 2019, p. 2.

[31] Human Rights Watch, *"I Saw It With My Own Eyes": Abuses by Chinese Security Forces in Tibet, 2008–2010*, July 21, 2010, p. 17; Human Rights Watch, *"Break Their Lineages, Break Their Roots": China's Crimes Against Humanity Targeting Uyghurs and Other Turkic Muslims*, April 19, 2021.

[32] "Xi Signs Order to Confer Honorary Title on Xinjiang Anti-Terrorist Squadron," *Xinhua*, July 5, 2021.

of Taiwan's population to prepare to resist an eventual Chinese invasion.[33] Another vulnerability lies in the risks of escalation from any clash near a border area, including the potential for inadvertent escalation that draws in U.S. military forces on China's borders to support an ally (e.g., Japan) or partner (e.g., India). Chinese misjudgment could thus result in a widening war that involves direct conventional combat with U.S. military forces.

With forces already fighting, the danger is higher for the economy, civilian casualties, and military casualties. There is also the danger of strategic blowback. Even a relatively successful border action could result in greater anti-China sentiment and higher defense budgets in surrounding countries. Tactical success on the battlefield could result in the formation of an anti-China coalition.

Finally, any efforts by the PLA to further punish ethnic minorities within its borders to prevent potential foreign interference is likely to generate additional reputational damage for China. This damage could make fence-sitting countries less likely to support (or at least acquiesce to) Chinese demands for external backing of its efforts in the broader low-intensity conflict.

Defensive Mission 3: Deter and Defeat Externally Backed Threats to Chinese Overseas Interests

China's overseas interests have grown extensively in recent decades, and Chinese leadership has expressed concern that these overseas investments and workers remain vulnerable to foreign interference.[34] Chinese companies have spent billions of dollars on major infrastructure projects around the world, many of which are in highly vulnerable or volatile regions along China's BRI routes.[35] Beijing's fears about the vulnerability of these interests to foreign interference would almost certainly be heightened in a scenario of low-intensity war with the United States. The PLA's contributions to these efforts would likely focus on China's immediate periphery in the Indo-Pacific and secure its broader interests in Europe, Africa, the Middle East, and the Americas.

We assess that this mission carries two specific tasks for the PLA: (1) efforts to degrade or destroy potential externally backed threats from nonstate actors or proxies and (2) efforts to protect key Chinese infrastructure abroad from sabotage. These tasks are summarized in Table 3.4.

---

[33] Lily Kuo, "Taiwan Election: Tsai Ing-Wen Wins Landslide in Rebuke to China," *The Guardian*, January 11, 2020. See also, "Strengthening Taiwan's Resistance," editorial, *Wall Street Journal*, July 22, 2021.

[34] State Council Information Office, *China's Military Strategy*, May 27, 2015.

[35] Boston University Global Development Policy Center, "China's Overseas Development Finance Database," last updated January 23, 2023; Oliver Cuenca, "Ethiopia-Djibouti Line Reports Reduced Revenue Due to Vandalism," *International Railway Journal*, December 16, 2020; Helena Legarda and Meia Nouwens, *Guardians of the Belt and Road: The Internationalization of China's Private Security Companies*, Mercator Institute for China Studies, August 16, 2018.

TABLE 3.4

People's Liberation Army Tasks to Deter and Defeat Externally Backed Threats to Overseas Interests (Low-Intensity Conflict Defensive Mission 3)

Tasks	Chinese Forces	Execution	Coordination with Nonmilitary Assets
Task 1: Degrade or destroy potential externally backed nonstate actor or proxy threats	• PLA (all services) • PLA SOF • PLA techs • PLASSF • PAP	• PLA technicians support arms sales and joint patrols with host nation • PAP supports counterterrorism operations with host-nation law enforcement • PLA joint operations against nonstate actors in border areas	• MFA • Host-nation intelligence and security, forces • PSCs
Task 2: Protect key infrastructure from sabotage or attack from foreign agents or armed groups	• PAP • PLAGF • PLA SOF • PLANMC	• PAP patrol areas near critical infrastructure • Local forces cooperate with PLA to protect assets • PLA prepares for NEO of Chinese civilians	• MFA • PSCs • Host-nation intelligence and security forces

As a first task, the PLA could conduct combat operations against externally backed groups that threaten Chinese interests abroad during a low-intensity conflict. From China's perspective, the United States has a long history of supporting nonstate actors to achieve its military objectives around the world, from resistance fighters in Latin America during the Cold War to the Syrian Democratic Forces in the 2010s. Even during peacetime competition, Chinese leaders tend to see U.S. support behind many antiauthoritarian resistance groups around the world, whether that support is real or simply perceived, and closely associate nonviolent pro-democratic groups with the potential for "terrorism" and broader political turmoil.[36] The PLA's concern over the potential for the United States to leverage nonstate actors to target its interests abroad would only increase during a low-intensity conflict. The PLA has little experience conducting combat operations against nonstate groups around the world outside United Nations peacekeeping operations.[37] PLA SOF and PLAAF or PLAN long-range strike assets would likely take the lead in such a campaign, in coordination with local governments and militaries.

As a second task, the PLA would likely be directed to protect key infrastructure and Chinese civilian populations from sabotage or subversion. The PLA has already been tasked with conducting noncombatant evacuation operations to protect Chinese citizens and others

---

[36] Higgins, 2019; "National Security Office of Central Government Says U.S. Plotting to Wage 'Color Revolution' in Hong Kong," Xinhua, September 25, 2021; Wang Hongyi [王洪一], "The Influence of New Security Challenges in Africa on Sino-African Cooperation" [非洲安全新挑战及其对中非合作的影响], China Institute of International Studies [中国国际问题研究院], July 25, 20.

[37] Heath et al., 2021, pp. 67–68.

from civil wars or other crises.[38] The possibility of hostile externally backed attacks on these vulnerable interests would provide a strong motivation for military leaders to direct more operations to protect them, particularly if they were threatened in the context of a broader low-intensity conflict. Relevant tasks could include more patrols by PAP and PLAGF troops, increased deployments of rapid reaction forces (including PLA SOF), training and equipping of host-nation forces, and higher levels of surveillance and reconnaissance in high-threat areas.

To improve its ability to deter strikes on its overseas interests, the PLA would likely need to improve its logistical, global-basing, and deep-strike capabilities.[39] Beijing prefers to work through host-nation law enforcement, military forces, or locally recruited security contractors.[40] In a low-intensity conflict with the United States, the PAP (including its associated SOF units) could play an increased role abroad because of its expertise in internal security missions. The PLAN, PLAAF, PLAJLSF, PLAGF, and PLANMC could also be given major responsibilities for carrying out relevant tasks. The military's involvement would complement civilian-led efforts by the MFA, civilian intelligence and security forces, and the UFWD.

A major vulnerability for the PLA's execution of this set of tasks lies in the limitations of its force projection capabilities. The PLA would likely be severely stressed if directed to carry out major combat operations outside China's immediate periphery, even if directed only against a nonstate actor. Countries could fear U.S. reprisals for supporting Chinese war efforts, especially given the PLA's limited ability to protect them. These difficulties are greatly compounded by China's reliance on friendly local governments to aid or at least host any PLA units tasked with protecting overseas people or infrastructure, suggesting that the PLA would face difficulties operating in semipermissive or denied environments. The weaknesses and limitations of client militaries could also prove a burden on Chinese efforts to carry out combined operations to protect its people or the interests of a client state.

Moreover, China's BRI infrastructure is often highly vulnerable, consisting of long transportation lines or large fixed facilities that could be quite difficult to defend against external threats. Damage to high-value infrastructure (such as factories, facilities, and ports) could be substantial. Military and civilian casualties from fighting and the spread of civil conflict or an aggravation of nontraditional threats could also accelerate.

---

[38] Shannon Tiezzi, "Chinese Nationals Evacuate Yemen on PLA Navy Frigate," *The Diplomat*, March 30, 2015.

[39] Liu Kun [刘昆], "Should We Take America's Gun? An Analysis of Chinese Military Interference in Iraq" [接过美国的枪? 中国武力干涉伊拉克前景分析], *Global Times* [环球], June 19, 2014.

[40] Note that China could develop a more advanced private military or private security company ecosystem, but most Chinese companies or projects rely on local militias, local law enforcement, or international (non-Chinese) security companies. See Alessandro Arduino, "China's Private Security Companies: The Evolution of a New Security Actor," Nadège Rolland, ed., *Securing the Belt and Road Initiative: China's Evolving Military Engagement Along the Silk Roads*, National Bureau of Asian Research, September 3, 2019, pp. 98–100.

There is also the risk that fighting in another country could spur political backlash and resistance to the PLA's presence. In some regions, Chinese investment has already sparked popular resentment and even armed resistance, which could prove far more dangerous in a low-intensity conflict than in peacetime.[41]

Defensive Mission 4: Defend China's Influence, Access, Partnerships, and Narrative from Subversion from External Threats

At present, the task of promoting Chinese influence in potential partner states abroad falls primarily to China's civilian government agencies and state-owned corporations, but the PLA does play a significant and growing role. Recent CCP documents call on the PLA to take a more active part in Chinese foreign policy work.[42] In a low-intensity war, the Chinese military would likely take more-active measures to protect both its own interests and those of key partners around the world. These missions would likely focus on China's immediate periphery in the Indo-Pacific and broader influence in Europe, Africa, the Middle East, and the Americas—Regions 2 and 3 as shown in our geographic laydown.

To accomplish this defensive mission in a low-intensity conflict, we assess that the PLA would likely perform two related tasks: defeat any U.S. efforts to subvert China's military partnerships and support China's client states in any wars against U.S.-backed proxy forces (Table 3.5).

The turn to greater involvement in the security of other countries would mark a dramatic change in Chinese foreign policy. Since the end of the Cold War, the PLA has avoided involvement in international conflicts even when violence threatens the security of partner nations.[43] When faced with regional rivalries or crises, China's strategy has generally been to avoid taking sides and seek to minimize any damage to trade or investment.[44] Because both sides in a given conflict are often eager to continue to benefit from economic ties with China, the conflict could leave both sides so weakened that it harms China's economic interests. Furthermore, Chinese scholars have noted the challenges faced by the United States in Vietnam, Iraq, and Afghanistan and are eager to avoid being drawn into open-ended foreign conflicts.[45]

---

[41] S. Khan Islamabad, "Can Pakistan Secure Chinese Investment in Balochistan?" Deutsche Welle, July 14, 2021.

[42] Office of the Secretary of Defense, 2021, p. 129.

[43] Note, for example, China's lack of any major involvement in the Syrian Civil War, Russia's confrontation with NATO over Ukraine, or Venezuela's low-level border conflict with Colombia. See International Crisis Group, *Disorder on the Border: Keeping the Peace Between Colombia and Venezuela*, December 14, 2020.

[44] Eyck Freymann, "Influence Without Entanglement in the Middle East," *Foreign Policy*, February 25, 2021, pp. 3–4.

[45] Freymann, 2021; Liu Kun, 2014. Note that in its most recent large scale war, the 1979 invasion of Vietnam, China very carefully limited the scope of its operations to avoid a Soviet response. See Zhang Xiaoming,

TABLE 3.5

People's Liberation Army Tasks to Defend Chinese Influence, Partners, Access, and Narratives from External Threats (Low-Intensity Conflict Defensive Mission 4)

Tasks	Chinese Forces	Execution	Coordination: Nonmilitary Assets
Task 1: Defeat U.S. efforts to subvert military partnerships	• PLA (all services) • PAP • CCG	• Intelligence, military diplomacy, joint exercises, and engagements to identify and counter U.S. influence operations	• Host-nation military • SOEs (for military equipment and finance) • MFA • Embassies • UFWD • Civilian intelligence
Task 2: Support client military in proxy wars against U.S.-backed partners	• PLA (all services) • PAP	• Provide arms, training, and intelligence; joint combat operations support; long-range tactical or strategic strikes; or counterinsurgency operations support	• Host-nation military • MFA • Embassies • UFWD • Civilian intelligence

However, China's foreign policy could change if Beijing and Washington entered a state of hostilities. The buildup of antagonistic coalitions would, in some ways. accelerate nascent trends. The United States already works to exclude Chinese information technology and other infrastructure wherever it can and encourages its allies to restrict Chinese investment. The United States is also building coalitions to balance against Chinese power through the Quadrilateral Security Dialogue and Australia-United Kingdom-United States.[46] China's relationships with Russia and Iran—both of which share resentment toward the United States—have deepened as well. Some Chinese scholars advocate the formation of alliances or the use of buffer states against U.S. power. For example, some Chinese scholars have argued that China should do what is necessary in a Korean conflict to protect the continued existence of North Korea as a buffer state.[47] China also relies on friendly governments in Central Asia to tamp down extremist movements that could otherwise metastasize into China's own western regions and that might fight to protect those governments should they be threatened. Small

---

"Deng Xiaoping and China's Decision to Go to War with Vietnam," *Journal of Cold War Studies*, Vol. 12, No. 3, Summer 2010.

[46] Makiko Yamazaki, David Kirton, and Ryan Woo, "U.K. Asks Japan for Huawei Alternatives in 5G Networks: Nikkei," Reuters, July 18, 2020; Leo Kelion, "Huawei 5G Kit Must be Removed from U.K. by 2027," BBC News, July 14, 2020.

[47] "China Must Be Ready for Worsened North Korea Ties," *Global Times*, April 27, 2017; Shi Yinhong, "Painful Lessons, Reversing Practices: China Facing North Korea since 2003," in Carla P. Freeman, ed., *China and North Korea*, Palgrave McMillan, 2015.

PLA contingents have deployed to friendly countries to keep tabs on conflicts that China also fears could spread into its own restive Western regions.[48]

There are two tasks the PLA could be expected to carry out. To protect military partnerships from subversion, China's military could carry out a variety of engagement activities, intelligence collection, and influence operations to identify U.S.-backed actors who seek to discredit those partnerships. These activities could involve efforts by attachés in partner countries from each of the PLA's services or physical operations by the PAP on the ground or the CCG in maritime domains. These efforts would likely be coordinated with host nation military partners, Chinese SOEs operating in partner countries, and nonmilitary Chinese actors such as the UFWD, the MFA, and the Ministry of State Security (MSS).

A second task might be for the PLA to support partner militaries in proxy fights with externally backed adversaries. This support might take the form of arms sales, advice, and assistance by PLA technicians and specialists. In some cases, this support might not be sufficient for the partner military's victory. If one of China's existing partner states appeared to be failing, especially at the hands of an adversary backed by the United States, Chinese leaders could direct the PLA to get involved in a more robust manner. China could send PSCs, along with PAP, PLA SOF, PLAGF, and PLANMC forces to shore up the client state.

If the threat faced by China's partner regime is internal, PSCs and the PAP could play a prominent role working with local military and police forces to protect key government personnel and facilities and suppress any protests or demonstrations.[49] The PLAAF or PLANMC could also participate in operations if a friendly government faced overthrow via coup, popular uprising, or insurgency. If extended counterinsurgency operations are needed, the PLAGF and PAP would form the backbone of any Chinese force that augmented partner troops. The MPS, MSS, and other government agencies would also likely provide support through intelligence operations. Even in a low-intensity war, China is likely to continue to prefer the use of host nation security forces wherever possible and would probably deploy PLA ground troops only when local forces prove utterly inadequate or other options have been exhausted. Similar standards apply should a state critical to Chinese security be threatened by a regional rival. In this case, PLARF, PLAAF, and PLAN long-range fires might provide China with a useful means of protecting its partner without involving ground troops.

Major vulnerabilities for China in the execution of both tasks include the lack of power projection capabilities and the risk that military action to support a partner nation could deepen into a quagmire. Beijing's desire to demonstrate its credibility as a partner could incentivize it to deepen a military commitment that proves extremely costly in terms of military and civilian casualties, disruptions to the security environment, and, perhaps, disruptions to economic interests.

---

[48] Akil and Shaar, 2021; Sheena Chestnut Greitens, *Dealing with Demand for China's Global Surveillance Exports*, Brookings Institution, April 2020, p. 1; Gerry Shih, "In Central Asia's Forbidding Highlands, a Quiet Newcomer: Chinese Troops," *Washington Post*, February 18, 2019.

[49] Wuthnow, 2019. p. 22.

Another vulnerability stems from the possible increase in antagonism toward Beijing among disaffected populations in the partner nation. The spread of violence would likely result in casualties among the local populace and disruptions to their livelihoods. China's reputation as a champion of the right of developing countries to exist free from military intervention by major powers would suffer a severe blow as well.

Finally, the risk of escalation to include a greater U.S. military presence cannot be discounted. Depending on the nature of the proxy conflict, Beijing could misjudge U.S. commitment and find itself trapped in a situation of escalating violence that begins to involve U.S. forces. Alternatively, Beijing could forgo a military intervention to support a partner facing instability out of fear of such escalation, missing an opportunity to bolster its relationships abroad.

People's Liberation Army Offensive Missions in a Low-Intensity Conflict

In addition to missions and tasks to protect Chinese interests, Beijing would likely direct the PLA to carry out a variety of missions and tasks designed to degrade U.S. ability and willingness to sustain the war effort. Offensive operations carry high risks, but Beijing would certainly consider opportunities to conduct the offensive actions that it deems necessary to secure victory. The following sections review four offensive missions for the PLA, and a set of likely tasks for various PLA forces to accomplish those missions.

Offensive Mission 1: Undermine and Threaten Government, Basic Security, and Social System of the United States and Its Allies

As part of a low-intensity war, PLA forces could step up information and cyber operations to demoralize the societies of, and gradually increase domestic pressure against the governments of, the United States and its allies and partners in the Indo-Pacific, Regions 2 and 4 in our geographic laydown.

In a low-intensity war with the United States, we assess that China could look to accomplish two specific tasks to undermine and threaten internal domestic cohesion within the United States and its partner nations as a coercive tool: potential cyber operations against key infrastructure and subversive efforts to foment domestic unrest (Table 3.6).

As a first task, the CCP could look to the PLA to prepare cyberstrike options against vulnerable U.S. infrastructure. Power grids, financial networks, and other key infrastructure could be surveilled, and vulnerabilities could be identified for potential strikes. In a low-intensity war, fears of escalation would probably incentivize Beijing to refrain from ordering cyberattacks on U.S. civilian infrastructure, but the PLASSF could be expected to develop options and signal the willingness to use the weapons as deterrent or retaliatory options in the event that the United States initiated such attacks.

TABLE 3.6

People's Liberation Army Tasks to Undermine and Threaten U.S. and Allied Governments, Security, Societies (Low-Intensity Conflict Offensive Mission 1)

Tasks	Chinese Forces	Execution	Coordination with Nonmilitary Assets
Task 1. Prepare CONUS cyber strike options	• PLASSF • PLA intelligence • PLARF • PLAN • PLAAF	• Develop target sets, develop access to networks and facilities • Deploy surveillance hardware, recruit U.S.-based agents	• UFWD • Civilian intelligence and security services • MFA
Task 2. Conduct subversion and foment domestic unrest in United States and allied countries	• PLASSF • PLA SOF	• Information operations; clandestine operations to provide arms, supplies, and funds for opposition groups • Disinformation campaigns, sabotage, covert operations	• UFWD • Civilian intelligence and security services • MFA

As a second task, Beijing could direct the PLA to execute specific steps against the United States and its allies that foment domestic unrest as a coercive tool to limit U.S. escalation during a low-intensity war. The CCP's extensive efforts to demoralize and subvert the government of Tsai Ing-Wen in Taiwan offers a precedent for what such actions could look like in the United States and its allied and partner nations. The Taiwan campaign has involved large-scale disinformation efforts, an uptick in cyberattacks on the Taiwanese government, economic pressure on companies that support Tsai, threats, and military intimidation.[50] It has also involved clandestine and overt support for her domestic political opponents.[51] Through these efforts, China seeks to convince the Taiwanese people that their government in general and Tsai's party in particular are incompetent and overly partisan, and that resisting unification with the mainland is futile and dangerous.[52]

Operations against the U.S. homeland, or against other countries contesting China as part of the broader low-intensity conflict, would represent an expansion of existing Chinese political efforts to undermine enemies of the CCP and build front groups in many countries.[53] Where opportunities present themselves in U.S. allied or partner countries featuring internal

---

[50] Joshua Kurlantzick, "How China Is Interfering in Taiwan's Election," Council on Foreign Relations, November 7, 2019; Debby Wu, "China Targets Corporate Backers of Taiwan's Ruling Party," Bloomberg, November 22, 2021.

[51] Kurlantzick, 2019.

[52] Scott W. Harold, Nathan Beauchamp-Mustafaga, and Jeffrey W. Hornung, *Chinese Disinformation Efforts on Social Media*, RAND Corporation, RR-4373/3-AF, 2021.

[53] Anne-Marie Brady, "New Zealand's Quiet China Shift," *The Diplomat*, July 2020; Amy Searight, "Countering China's Influence Operations: Lessons from Australia," Center for Strategic and International Studies, May 8, 2020.

stress and the potential for fragmentation, China might even seek to train and equip client nonstate actors in an effort to subvert the legitimacy of such governments through sabotage and subversion. CCP organs such as the UFWD, Central Propaganda Department, and MSS would play a major role in political subversion campaigns.[54] At least two CCP organs already seem to be operating covert social media campaigns semi-independently against Taiwan.[55]

One key Chinese vulnerability in these tasks is the danger of escalation. Even if the CCP views disruptive cyberattacks on U.S. infrastructure as a reasonable retaliation for cyberattacks that they believe originated from the United States, the United States could respond to such attacks with subversive efforts of its own, or even conventional or nuclear force depending on the severity of the attack. The result could be devastation to the country's infrastructure or major damage to the economy's prospects. The possibility of civilian casualties cannot be discounted if the electric grid, air traffic control, and other key infrastructure were disrupted.

Another potential vulnerability in the execution of such tasks lies in the challenge of gaining access to key targets. Efforts by PLA SOF or PLA cyber forces to gain physical or virtual access to targeted populations or critical infrastructure are vulnerable to disruption by internal security measures in U.S. allied or partner nations, and the PLA has little proven ability to operate in denied environments for such missions. Another vulnerability lies in the inherent risk of backlash if China's role in fomenting such unrest were to be discovered. Disclosure of such Chinese malign influence in the politics and society of other societies could drive those countries to adopt policies hostile to Chinese interests or deepen cooperation with the United States. The result could be a further escalation of hostilities into a widening war.

Offensive Mission 2: Threaten Territory and Sovereignty Occupied by U.S. Allies and Partners

In a low-intensity conflict against the United States, China's government might be more willing to authorize operations that challenge the sovereign control of territory held by U.S. allies and partners along China's periphery and throughout the broader Indo-Pacific. The purpose of these efforts would be to weaken the rival state and demonstrate Chinese superiority over U.S. power. China's primary target is thus not the United States directly but U.S. allies or partners along the periphery. Chinese scholars have long accused the United States of encouraging rival claimants to challenge Beijing's sovereignty over the East and South China seas and the Indian border.[56]

---

[54] Harold, Beauchamp-Mustafaga, and Hornung, 2021, p. 36.

[55] Harold, Beauchamp-Mustafaga, and Hornung, 2021, p. 37.

[56] Tania Branigan, "China Lambasts U.S. over South China Sea Row," *The Guardian*, August 6, 2022; Wajahat Khan and Ken Moriyasu, "U.S. Arms Sales in Indo-Pacific Pick Up as China Tensions Build," *Nikkei Asia*, August 21, 2020.

We assess that such a directive to the PLA would focus on one core task involving PLA efforts to employ limited military force to challenge rival claims to contested territory either directly or indirectly (through a partner) (Table 3.7).

In this context, Chinese military forces could collaborate with paramilitary forces, such as the CCG or a Chinese PSC, to contend for disputed territory or support a partner's effort to secure territory within a neighboring country. Civilian entities, such as the MFA, propaganda-media, and UFWD, could provide political cover and advance legal and political arguments in favor of Chinese goals. A precedent might be seen in the allegations that China supports armed antigovernment tribal groups in Myanmar.[57] This support likely includes weapons, might include training by PLA personnel, and seems to have been instrumental in preventing the central government from asserting control over the region controlled by the pro-China United Wa State Army.[58] Beijing could seek to replicate this success elsewhere in the event of a broader low-intensity clash with the United States, creating armed pro-China enclaves in neighboring states as a coercive tool to punish rival states partnered with the United States, or to extend U.S. resources by creating multiple, competing dilemmas. The Chinese have long accused the United States and its allies of supporting separatist nonstate actors within Chinese territory, and the CCP could decide that a similar approach is fair play in supporting separatist groups in the countries of key U.S. partners. As an example, Chinese universities, media, and think tanks have already forged ties with Okinawa independence groups in Japan.[59]

The principal vulnerability lies in the danger of escalation from a low-intensity to a high-intensity conflict. A rival state might respond to Chinese gray-zone and paramilitary attacks

TABLE 3.7

People's Liberation Army Tasks to Threaten the Sovereignty, Territory of the U.S. Allies and Partners (Low-Intensity Conflict Offensive Mission 2)

Tasks	Chinese Forces	Execution	Coordination with Nonmilitary Assets
Task 1: PLA directly challenges or supports partner who contends for territory in U.S.-backed partner state	• PLA (all services) • PLA intelligence • CCG • PLASSF	• PLA joint operations to contest territory; arms sales, technical assistance, ISR and SOF support to client militaries fighting U.S.-backed partner over territory	• MFA • Embassies • UFWD • Partner-nation military forces • PMC • Civilian intelligence

[57] Prabin Kalita, "Ulfa-I Operating from Base in China: Centre Tells Tribunal," *The Times of India*, October 4, 2020; Alessandro Rippa and Martin Saxer, "Mong La: Business as Usual in the China-Myanmar Borderlands," *East Asian History and Culture Review*, No. 19, June 2016, pp. 249–250; Janes, "United Wa State Army," *Jane's World Insurgency and Terrorism*, May 16, 2019.

[58] Janes, "Army of Autonomy: The Rise of the United Wa State Army," *Jane's Defense Weekly*, January 8, 2016.

[59] "Chinese Groups Seen Forging Ties with Okinawa Independence Activists," *Japan Times*, December 27, 2016; Higgins, 2019.

with conventional forces, which could escalate the conflict. U.S. conventional forces could enter the conflict as well, raising the risk of a broader conventional war.

A second possible vulnerability concerns the political fear of operational failure, although Beijing could become more risk tolerant in a systemic low-intensity conflict with the United States. The military risks of operating further from Chinese shores could leave involved PLA forces exposed to greater threats and physical risks during a low-intensity conflict, especially in more-distant areas such as the Spratly Islands in the South China Sea or in distant locations associated with major BRI investments. Although the PLA is improving its global-basing and C2 infrastructure, long-distance logistical and command links could be vulnerable to disruption, and units operating far from mainland China might need to deploy without adequate force protection. The political dangers of operational failure in such a conflict could be severe. Chinese leaders could face significant domestic backlash if operations led to shocking levels of casualties or humiliating failures.

Another potential vulnerability for China in executing this task might be in the damage to China's reputation from such activities, as Beijing would likely be portrayed as the aggressor and in violation of its oft-stated belief in nonintervention in the internal affairs of foreign countries. The result could be a further deterioration in the international security environment as more nations join the United States in an anti-China coalition.

Offensive Mission 3: Threaten Key Overseas Interests of the United States and Its Allies

Although official Chinese writings on overseas interests overwhelmingly focus on China's own interests and how they could be protected, China could instead seek to hold vulnerable U.S. or allied infrastructure at risk around the world in a low-intensity conflict through acts of sabotage or nonkinetic methods, such as cyberstrikes. These activities would likely occur in the Indo-Pacific (Region 2) and Europe, Africa, the Middle East, and the Americas (Region 3).

We assess that this mission has one primary task, which is to damage the critical infrastructure and assets of partner nations abroad (Table 3.8).

TABLE 3.8

People's Liberation Army Tasks to Threaten U.S. and Allied Overseas Interests (Low-Intensity Conflict Offensive Mission 3)

Tasks	Chinese Forces	Execution	Coordination: Nonmilitary Assets
Task 1: Damage externally backed partner country infrastructure, assets	• PLA SOF • PLASSF	• Carry out clandestine sabotage of key infrastructure targets • Cyberattacks on infrastructure	• MFA • Civilian intelligence • MSS • Partner countries

In such a scenario, the PLA would likely rely on SOF or cyber forces for sabotage. Such attacks could be carried out as part of an enhanced subversion campaign, to degrade America's ability to move forces globally, or as a response to U.S. or allied attacks on Chinese infrastructure. PLASSF might try, for example, to disrupt U.S. military logistics networks through cyber means. PLA SOF could also attempt to carry out clandestine acts of sabotage to ruin U.S. military fuel depots, maintenance facilities, supply lines, or communications infrastructure in forward locations.

A major vulnerability in Chinese military efforts to carry out this task rests in the potential for escalation, principally in the form of retaliation. Because of the PLA's limited ability to protect its overseas interests, an action to threaten the citizens or assets of the United States or any of its allies could endanger exposed Chinese citizens and assets abroad. Washington could view such attacks as highly aggressive and order robust retaliatory measures against highly vulnerable assets and infrastructure outside the mainland, resulting in serious economic damage and potential loss of life.

An additional vulnerability is Beijing's lack of proven ability to operate in denied environments to conduct such sabotage operations, either unilaterally or through a partner force. This vulnerability is compounded by China's limited experience with power projection far beyond China's borders, its risk avoidance with regard to potential PLA casualties, and its lack of overseas bases and capable military allies.

Local economies that are dependent on U.S. infrastructure struck by China could turn hostile against Beijing as well. The result could be the strengthening of international support for an anti-China coalition.

Offensive Mission 4: Undermine U.S. Influence, Alliances and Partnerships, Access, and Narrative

China has long considered the U.S. alliance system (especially in East Asia) to be a threat to its security and sought to weaken that system—or at least prevent it from getting any stronger. A low-intensity conflict could greatly accelerate these efforts and expand to the Indo-Pacific (Region 2) and Europe, Africa, the Middle East, and the Americas (Region 3).

We assess that this offensive mission could include three potential tasks: eroding U.S. military partnerships and access, eroding confidence in U.S. military power, and potentially supporting the overthrow of U.S.-backed regimes (Table 3.9).

As a first task, the PLA could take a more direct role in persuading a country to abandon its alliance or partnership with the United States. The principal means to achieve this would likely involve a mix of incentives and threats. Working with civilian authorities, PLA officials could employ military diplomacy to incentivize cooperation. At the same time, PLASSF units could spread propaganda and disinformation about the United States. PLA and civilian authorities could identify and back favored actors to gain power and support nonkinetic and kinetic options to eliminate key U.S. supporters.

TABLE 3.9

People's Liberation Army Tasks to Undermine U.S. Influence, Alliances and Partnerships, Access, and Narrative (Low-Intensity Conflict Offensive Mission 4)

Tasks	Chinese Forces	Execution	Coordination: Nonmilitary Assets
Task 1: Erode U.S. military influence, alliances and partnerships, and access	• PLASSF • PLA intelligence agencies • PLA SOF	• Military diplomacy, disinformation campaigns, identification and funding of local political proxies, exfiltration and leaking of information, identification and harassment of spreaders of counternarratives, military intimidation	• MFA • UFWD • Civilian security and intelligence • Propaganda-media
Task 2: Erode confidence in U.S. power through military demonstrations	• PLAN • PLAAF • PLARF • PLAGF • PLA publicity organs	• Major naval exercises, including amphibious exercises; weapons tests, demonstrations of military might	• MFA • UFWD • Civilian security and intelligence • Propaganda-media
Task 3: Support overthrow of U.S.-backed regimes (as needed)	• PLAGF • PLA SOF • PLA intelligence agencies	• Clandestine distribution of arms, supplies, or funds • Set-up and staffing of training camps • Provision battlefield intelligence • Potential PLA invasion	• MSS • UFWD • Civilian security and intelligence

Second, PLA sources could aim to undermine the appeal of the United States as a security partner. It could do this through propaganda, disinformation, and demonstrations of Chinese military prowess, such as exercises, weapon tests, and other demonstrations.[60] China has frequently used such methods to intimidate and coerce Taiwan, in part as a way of warning Taiwan against deepening its military ties with the United States.[61] These exercises generally involve the demonstration of capabilities that the PLA likely considers to be especially intimidating, including amphibious invasion and naval or air operations to isolate the island.[62] Chinese demonstrations of long-range antiship ballistic missiles and

---

[60] Bryan Clark, Timothy A. Walton, Melinda Tourangeau, and Steve Tourangeau, *The Invisible Battlefield: A Technology Strategy for U.S. Electromagnetic Spectrum Superiority*, Hudson Institute, March 10, 2021, p. 4; Zhang Junshe [张军社], "'Three Armies and Four Seas' Drills: Deterring Those Who Conspire Against Us" [三军四海"大演习 : 威慑图谋不轨之国], *People's Daily* [人民日报], July 29, 2014.

[61] John Xie, "China Is Increasing Taiwan Airspace Incursions," *Voice of America*, January 6, 2021.

[62] Kristen Huang, "Chinese Military Drills Simulate Amphibious Landing and Island Seizure in Battle Conditions," *South China Morning Post*, July 28, 2021; Liu Xuanzun, "PLA Prepared as U.S., Secessionists Provoke," *Global Times*, April 8, 2021.

long-range airstrikes on U.S. carrier groups might also be read as efforts to sway minds throughout Asia.[63]

Finally, in extreme circumstances, the PLA might be called on to support the violent overthrow of another government that is deemed to be especially threatening to Chinese security or interests. Throughout the Cold War, all major powers, including China, participated in such actions, and a low-intensity conflict that hardened strategic alignments and made U.S. allies seem especially threatening could lead China to overcome its long aversion to regime change operations. For example, China supported the Khmer Rouge against Vietnam in the 1970s.[64] Similarly, Beijing could provide arms or funding to local violent nonstate actors seeking to resist or overthrow the target regime, send so-called volunteers in the PLA SOF or PLAGF to directly support rebels, or launch a full-scale invasion of regimes it believed endangered China's safety. Although Chinese-led regime change operations might be an unlikely course of action at present, China's willingness to use force could change in the event of an ongoing low-intensity war with the United States.

China faces several major vulnerabilities in the execution of such operations. One risk is operational failure. In particular, combat operations to support a client state carry a high risk of botched military performance for a largely untested PLA. Countries could question China's military capacity if the PLA's performance proves underwhelming.

Escalation into a broader war is another major risk. PLA combat operations against a U.S. ally or significant partner could invite direct intervention by U.S. forces. Even if U.S. forces did not get involved, Beijing faces the risk that the low-intensity conflict could turn into a quagmire that imposes large costs in life and resources.

Another vulnerability lies in domestic or strategic backlash. Evidence of Chinese involvement in another country's internal conflict could generate domestic opposition back home in China, especially if such involvement resulted in major PLA casualties or imposed heavy resource costs, as happened to the United States in the Vietnam War and in other Cold War interventions. Moreover, successful PLA intimidation operations could cause a target country to seek even closer cooperation with the United States. The United States might engage in its own demonstrations, possibly with the participation of the ally or partner in question, to show its ability and willingness to intervene in a conflict with China. To avoid a quagmire, China might try to operate through proxies, such as PSCs or militia groups, but these operations carry their own risks, and the PLA's limited prior experience operating in denied environments or in foreign languages could complicate its chances of success. Disclosure of

---

[63] Kathrin Hille and Demetri Sevastopulo, "Chinese Warplanes Simulated Attacking U.S. Carrier Near Taiwan," *Financial Times*, January 29, 2021.

[64] See for example, Chenyi Wang, "The Chinese Communist Party's Relationship with the Khmer Rouge in the 1970s: An Ideological Victory and a Strategic Failure," working paper, Wilson Center, December 2018.

Chinese involvement could result in reputational blowback that might complicate Chinese decisionmaking and its influence on other nations.[65]

Overview of the People's Liberation Army's Vulnerabilities in Low-Intensity Conflict

This chapter has provided an analysis of potential PLA missions to support a hypothetical low-intensity conflict with the United States and its allies and partners. Our list of PLA missions and tasks provides a framework through which U.S. military planners can understand the wide variety of activities that China's military would likely undertake to weaken U.S. power in an indirect way. Beijing would likely not authorize hostile actions by PLA forces against uniformed U.S. troops. However, other hostile acts could be authorized against partner forces aligned with the United States. China could also carry out preparations and plans for more-hostile actions against the United States in anticipation of possible escalation.

This analysis derives various hypothesized vulnerabilities in the PLA's ability to successfully execute these missions in pursuit of China's potential strategic objectives in a low-intensity war. Table 3.10 summarizes these assessed vulnerabilities for the PLA that are associated with each mission.

TABLE 3.10

Low-Intensity Conflict Scenario: People's Liberation Army Missions and Potential Vulnerabilities

PLA Mission	Potential Vulnerabilities
Defensive Mission 1: Deter and defeat externally backed threats to CCP, basic security, and socialist system	• Difficulties of securing soft targets • Burden of heavy security that could impair economy • Domestic discontent that could grow from heavy repression
Defensive Mission 2: Deter and defeat externally backed threats to China's territory, sovereignty, and national unity	• Unknown adequacy of PLA forces and execution of military operations • Risk of escalation and economic damage from aggressive measures to protect Chinese sovereignty claims • Hardened adversary popular resolve to resist Chinese coercion • Reputational blowback in fence-sitting countries
Defensive Mission 3: Deter and defeat externally backed threats to Chinese overseas interests	• Limited power projection capabilities that could be stressed in wartime • Heavy reliance on partners with limited warfighting capabilities, potential dependencies • Limited ability to defend against physical vulnerabilities to key infrastructure abroad • Potential for popular backlash and violence against Chinese presence or coercion

[65] Laura Silver, Kat Devlin, and Christine Huang, "Unfavorable Views of China Reach Historic Highs in Many Countries," Pew Research Center, October 6, 2020.

Table 3.10—Continued

PLA Mission	Potential Vulnerabilities
Defensive Mission 4: Defend China's influence, access, partnerships, and narrative from U.S. subversion attempts	• Lack of power projection capabilities • Risk of protracted involvement in supporting besieged partner nation • Risk of popular backlash from coercion to shore up political pressure • Risk of escalation that drives greater U.S. military involvement
Offensive Mission 1: Undermine and threaten government, basic security, and social system of United States and allies	• Risk of social and economic harm from like-for-like escalation • Limited ability to operate in nonpermissive environments • Risk of backlash from intrusive Chinese interference in domestic politics
Offensive Mission 2: Threaten the territory and sovereignty of U.S. allies	• Escalation risks from supporting threats to sovereignty of territory controlled by other countries, and ensuing instability • Risks to PLA forces conducting operations abroad, and sensitivity at home to PLA casualties • Danger of reputational damage from aggressive actions
Offensive Mission 3: Threaten overseas interests of the United States and its allies	• Limited ability to operate in denied environments or project power • Risk of retaliatory strikes against Chinese infrastructure • Reputational blowback on China in affected countries
Offensive Mission 4: Undermine U.S. influence, access, alliances and partnerships, and narrative	• Escalation risk inviting direct intervention by U.S. forces or protraction of conflict • Risk of reputational damage and reduced influence • Limited ability to operate through partners in nonpermissive environments or in foreign languages

These vulnerabilities provide a sense of the difficulties and potential pressure points that the PLA is likely to face in accomplishing its objectives in a low-intensity conflict and the challenges faced by CCP decisionmakers in leveraging the military instrument of power to achieve their objectives in a broader confrontation with the United States. Broadly speaking, these vulnerabilities can be summarized across the same five sets of vulnerabilities identified in our peacetime competition analysis with different focuses in a low-intensity conflict:

- **Domestic instability:** These vulnerabilities consist of the potential for PLA operations to exacerbate domestic instability in China. In low-intensity conflict, these vulnerabilities include the potential for rising discontent and opposition to CCP rule from military and civilian casualties, economic disruption and damage, and rising domestic oppression from heightened security measures. This vulnerability is particularly heightened in offensive missions for low-intensity conflict and in domestic missions focused on defending against externally backed threats to internal stability.
- **Escalation risk:** These vulnerabilities consist of PLA operations and activities to intensify conflict or damage China's economic prospects. In low-intensity conflict, they include the risk of direct conflict with U.S. forces, expansion of war into other domains and geographic areas beyond China's original intent, and the possibility that PLA forces

could be dragged into a protracted conflict or quagmire. Even low-intensity war could impose severe costs on the global economy and China's access to critical import and export markets. This type of vulnerability is exceedingly possible across most defensive and offensive PLA missions in this scenario.

- **Reputational risk:** These vulnerabilities arise from the potential for actions taken or inaction by the PLA to result in severe costs to China's reputation, influence, and appeal as a partner. In low-intensity conflict, vulnerabilities include the possibility that an anti-China coalition might form as a result of perceived aggressive actions by China, or that China's appeal as a security partner might diminish as a result of failures to effectively support its partners. This vulnerability is similarly applicable across most missions in this scenario, with the real possibility that China's security environment could be severely worsened in a low-intensity conflict.

- **Limited ability to support partners:** These vulnerabilities consist of limitations in the PLA's ability to assist partner forces abroad. In low-intensity conflict, vulnerabilities include the PLA's inability to rely on its partners to protect vulnerable Chinese infrastructure abroad and the PLA's limited ability to help partners overcome major warfighting gaps. These vulnerabilities are primarily applicable in those defensive and offensive missions at China's near periphery and further abroad.

- **Limited ability to project power:** These vulnerabilities consist of potential failures by the PLA to protect Chinese citizens and their assets abroad. In low-intensity conflict, they include limitations in the PLA's capabilities and experience sustaining major combat operations abroad for an extended period of time, its limited basing and logistics presence abroad, its limited ability to defend vulnerable soft targets abroad, and a lack of experience operating in nonpermissive environments. These vulnerabilities could be most acute in the beginning of a low-intensity war and in more-distant locations.

We reiterate that these vulnerabilities represent analytic hypotheses that are worthy of further research and validation. However, they do offer analytically informed baseline assessments intended to promote further thinking on ways to disrupt and counter Chinese strategies in a hypothetical low-intensity conflict with the United States.

Chapter 4 of this report focuses on the implications of this vulnerability analysis for potential U.S. military efforts to disrupt China's ability to leverage the PLA to achieve the China Dream.

Options for Disrupting the People's Liberation Army

In a companion report, we explore the potential for the U.S. military to frustrate adversary-preferred strategies by targeting adversary vulnerabilities and thus enable strategic disruption of adversary core interests short of war that sets favorable conditions for strategic gains by the United States.[1] In this chapter, we apply this concept for strategic disruption to the PLA's assessed vulnerabilities in the key competition and low-intensity conflict missions featured in Chapters 2 and 3 of this report. Specifically, we explore the potential for the United States to exploit these vulnerabilities to frustrate the PLA's preferred operational design for executing specific missions, thereby disrupting China's broader goals in leveraging the PLA to achieve core objectives short of high-intensity war.

We should make clear that this chapter does not assess the effectiveness of potential U.S. efforts to exploit PLA vulnerabilities, nor does it define the operational approach that U.S. forces would likely take to accomplish such objectives. Rather, it focuses on guiding future defense planning by understanding potential avenues through which the United States could pursue strategic disruption opportunities that frustrate the ability of CCP leadership to leverage the PLA to achieve national strategic objectives.

In the companion report, the concept of *strategic disruption* is defined as "set[ting] favorable conditions to achieve national objectives through deliberate efforts to delay, degrade, or deny an adversary's ability to achieve core interests via their own preferred courses of action."[2] The logic of this approach is summarized in Figure 4.1. In this concept,

> friendly forces conduct individual tactical actions, or a series of tactical actions as part of an operational-level campaign, that are designed to frustrate some aspect of an adversary's preferred strategy to achieve their core national interests. These disruptive campaigns do not need to produce strategic effects in and of themselves. Rather they are designed to delay, degrade, or deny an adversary's ability to achieve any number of broader diplomatic, informational, military, or economic (DIME) interests. Specifically, these disruptive campaigns are meant to impose costs or create dilemmas that limit an adver-

---

[1] See Robinson et. al, 2023.

[2] See Robinson et al., 2023, p. v, for an overview of this concept.

FIGURE 4.1

The Logic of Strategic Disruption

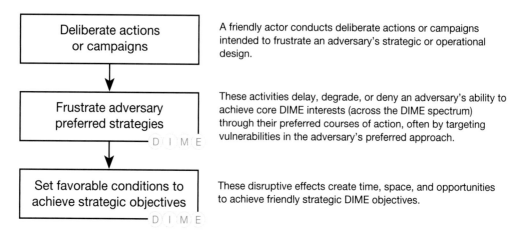

SOURCE: Reproduced from Robinson et al., 2023, p. vi.

sary's ability to achieve their core interests through preferred courses of action. This often involves efforts by the friendly actor to target underlying vulnerabilities in the adversary's preferred approach. Implicit in this approach is that the adversary's preferred course of action is the one assessed as most likely to achieve strategic objectives.[3]

Applying this concept to our current analysis of PLA missions and tasks can help reveal opportunities for the United States to disrupt efforts by CCP leadership to employ the PLA to achieve strategic objectives in peacetime competition and low-intensity conflict. Specifically, our analysis of the PLA's vulnerabilities in such scenarios identifies potential pressure points that the United States could leverage to frustrate the ability of the PLA to execute assigned missions.

Table 4.1 summarizes the five broad categories of PLA vulnerabilities that we have identified in our analysis of peacetime competition and low-intensity conflict missions. These vulnerabilities should not be seen as potential silver bullets that, if exploited, could lead to immediate mission failure by the PLA. Moreover, the CCP and PLA are likely to take steps to address these vulnerabilities in the coming years, particularly in regions of the world where U.S.-China competition becomes particularly acute.

These vulnerabilities are best understood as variables that affect either the PLA's ability to execute specific missions or the potential adverse effects of PLA operations. As a result, they represent a framework for understanding potential constraints on senior Chinese decision-makers in their ability to leverage the PLA to achieve national strategic objectives short of a large-scale high-intensity war and therefore opportunities for the United States to amplify,

---

[3] Robinson et al., 2023, p. vi.

TABLE 4.1

Potential PLA Vulnerabilities in Peacetime Competition and Low-Intensity Conflict

Category	Vulnerabilities in Peacetime Competition	Vulnerabilities in Low-Intensity Conflict
Domestic instability	• Economic, social, and ethnic unrest and inadequacy of legitimate channels to seek redress • Potential politicization of military • Sensitivity to PLA casualties	• Potential unrest from domestic civilian casualties, PLA casualties, economic hardship arising from conflict
Escalation risk	• Risk of escalation from aggressive assertion of sovereignty claims or attempts to undermine the United States and its allies or partners	• Risk that the conflict broadens to include U.S. forces or becomes a larger-scale war than Beijing intended • Potential economic disruptions to Chinese market access from broader instability • Risk that Chinese forces find themselves enmeshed in a protracted conflict
Reputational risk	• Overt aggression, covert interference, and domestic repression from China that can reduce its desirability as a partner • Inadequate support to a partner that damages China's appeal as partner • Coercion that hardens competitor or adversary resolve	• Weak ability to provide direct military to support to partners could reduce desirability as an ally • Perceptions of aggressive China could generate anti-China coalition
Limited ability to support partners	• Limited partner relationships • Unproven ability to enable partners • Limited experience operating in foreign languages • Limited impact of diplomacy and information operations on long-term partnerships	• PLA has limited ability to rely on partners to defend against vulnerable infrastructure, facilities abroad • Limited ability to support partners to overcome major warfighting gaps
Limited ability to project power	• Inadequate logistics to support operations far from the Chinese mainland • Limited ability to conduct major operations abroad • Limited overseas basing	• PLA is untested in large-scale combat operations and its military could fail on the battlefield • Inadequate logistics could endanger operations • Limited ability to defend vulnerable targets abroad or operate in nonpermissive environments

exacerbate, challenge, or disrupt such activities to limit the effectiveness of the PLA as an instrument of Chinese national power.

The first three categories of vulnerabilities focus on potential unintended but adverse consequences of PLA military actions that could create domestic instability in China, undue escalation or protraction, and broader reputational blowback in response to more-aggressive Chinese actions. These downstream potential risks of PLA operations are vulnerabilities to the extent that they are likely to affect the willingness of CCP leaders to leverage the PLA in the first place or constrain the flexibility with which the PLA is permitted to operate in ways that could limit its ability to achieve specific objectives.

The final two categories of vulnerabilities focus more on the potential weaknesses in the PLA's operational capabilities that could limit its effectiveness in conducting certain military operations abroad, particularly working alongside partners or projecting power far from the Chinese mainland. These limitations are vulnerabilities to the extent that they are also likely to affect the willingness of CCP leaders to task the PLA to achieve far-reaching or complex military objectives and will naturally limit the probability of PLA success on any given operation.

From a strategic disruption standpoint, each of these broad sets of vulnerabilities represent potential avenues through which the United States could frustrate China's strategic or operational designs, specifically to prevent CCP leaders from leveraging the PLA to conduct optimal, preferred approaches to achieving specific objectives in peacetime competition and low-intensity conflict.

The People's Liberation Army's Vulnerabilities to Strategic Disruption in Peacetime Competition

We first explore potential mechanisms through which the United States could leverage these vulnerabilities to attempt strategic disruption of the CCP's preferred approach of employing the PLA to achieve core national objectives in peacetime competition. Several caveats are worth emphasizing. China's government is aware of many of these vulnerabilities and is taking steps to address them, although progress has been uneven. Moreover, many of these assessed vulnerabilities for the PLA are most severe in regions of the world where the United States has fewer of its own national interests at stake, such as Africa. Nevertheless, Table 4.2 summarizes vulnerabilities associated with each of the four defensive and four offensive missions that we assess the PLA might be tasked to execute in peacetime competition with the United States.

We assess that the predominant vulnerability faced by CCP decisionmakers in employing the PLA to support peacetime competition objectives is the potential for reputational blowback from PLA overreach in conducting each of the offensive and defensive missions we analyzed in this report. Secondarily, the PLA is somewhat vulnerable to potential downstream consequences of creating domestic instability and escalation risk with the United States. The PLA is particularly vulnerable to limitations in its ability to support partners and project power abroad when defending or threatening overseas interests outside China's near abroad.

Per our underlying concept for strategic disruption, deliberate U.S. campaigns to disrupt the PLA in peacetime competition could focus on delaying, degrading, or denying China's achievement of its core interests by leveraging these vulnerabilities to frustrate CCP preferred strategies. This approach could take three broad forms.

TABLE 4.2

Peacetime Competition People's Liberation Army Missions and Potential Vulnerabilities

Mission	Domestic Instability	Escalation Risk	Reputational Risk	Limited Ability to Support Partners	Limited Ability to Project Power
Defensive Mission 1: Deter and defeat externally backed threats to CCP legitimacy	Yes	No	Yes	No	No
Defensive Mission 2: Defend China's territory and sovereignty	No	Yes	Yes	No	Yes
Defensive Mission 3: Defend Chinese overseas interests	Yes	No	Yes	Yes	Yes
Defensive Mission 4: Defend China's influence abroad	No	No	Yes	Yes	No
Offensive Mission 1: Undermine U.S. and partner legitimacy	No	No	Yes	No	No
Offensive Mission 2: Threaten U.S. partner territory and sovereignty	No	Yes	Yes	No	No
Offensive Mission 3: Threaten U.S. and partner overseas interests	No	No	Yes	Yes	Yes
Offensive Mission 4: Undermine U.S. influence abroad	No	No	Yes	No	No

First, the United States could seek to deter unwanted PLA actions from occurring by shaping Chinese perceptions of the potential adverse effects of those actions. This is particularly relevant for potential U.S. military efforts to deter Chinese aggression against the territorial claims of U.S. allies and partners in China's near periphery (Defensive Mission 2 and Offensive Mission 2). The United States could, for example, tie Chinese gray-zone coercion to stronger security cooperation with countries in the Asia Pacific to highlight the strategic costs of Chinese tactical gains. The United States could also link increased military presence in the region to Chinese coercion as another way to highlight the strategic costs of Chinese tactical gains.

Alternatively, the United States could exploit the adverse consequences of PLA actions after they occur to limit the CCP's desire to pursue similar efforts through the PLA in the future. This approach could be particularly effective for efforts to exploit the reputational blowback of potential PLA actions. These potential actions include China's internal efforts to deter externally backed threats to CCP legitimacy (Defensive Mission 1), undermine the legitimacy of the United States and its partners (Offensive Mission 1), or even undermine U.S. influence abroad (Offensive Mission 4). The United States could reveal and illuminate evidence of the PLA's role in such coercive activities as a means of complicating China's ability to build partnerships abroad, creating dilemmas for similar future coercion.

Finally, the United States could exploit specific PLA weaknesses in power projection and partner support to reduce the likelihood of PLA success in any given operation or incentivize CCP decisionmakers to rely on the PLA when other nonmilitary approaches would be more likely to succeed. This approach is particularly applicable to China's efforts to defend its overseas interests (Defensive Mission 3), defend its influence and narrative abroad (Defensive Mission 4), and even threaten U.S. and partner interests overseas (Offensive Mission 3). The United States could expand its security partnerships in countries with significant Chinese overseas economic interests to show direct contrast to the PLA's limited ability to provide comparable levels of support. The United States could also expand partnerships in areas where the PLA would face significant difficulties projecting its own power. This expansion could lead the CCP to pursue similar approaches to security cooperation, but these approaches are likely to be less effective at building partner relationships than Chinese economic outreach and could even create tensions if the approach is seen as overly aggressive or tied to efforts by China to counter the United States rather than to support a partner nation.

The People's Liberation Army's Vulnerabilities to Strategic Disruption in Low-Intensity Conflict

We next explore potential mechanisms through which the United States could leverage similar vulnerabilities to attempt strategic disruption of the CCP's preferred approach to employing the PLA to achieve core national objectives in a low-intensity conflict. Table 4.3 summarizes the four defensive and four offensive missions that we assess the PLA might be tasked with executing in a hypothetical low-intensity conflict with the United States, alongside those vulnerabilities that we hypothesize to be associated with each mission.

The risks and vulnerabilities for the PLA in such a scenario are multiplied relative to peacetime competition. Specifically, CCP decisionmakers are likely to have heightened fear of escalation in a war situation, as well as a fear of downstream effects of such actions on domestic instability within China. Similarly, China's limited proven ability to project power far abroad from the Chinese mainland and its limited ability to operate in nonpermissive environments for offensive missions are major vulnerabilities in a low-intensity conflict. The PLA's limited experience overseas and in enabling partners also leaves it vulnerable to failure in more-offensive missions to challenge U.S. interests and influence overseas.

Per our underlying concept for strategic disruption, deliberate U.S. campaigns to disrupt the PLA in low-intensity conflict could focus on delaying, degrading, or denying China's achievement of its core interests in pursuit of core national objectives. Unlike in peacetime

TABLE 4.3

Low-Intensity Conflict PLA Missions and Potential Vulnerabilities

Mission	Domestic Instability	Escalation Risk	Reputational Risk	Limited Ability to Support Partners	Limited Ability to Project Power
Defensive Mission 1: Deter and defeat externally backed threats to CCP legitimacy	Yes	No	No	No	Yes
Defensive Mission 2: Defend China's territory and sovereignty	No	Yes	Yes	No	Yes
Defensive Mission 3: Defend Chinese overseas interests	No	Yes	Yes	Yes	Yes
Defensive Mission 4: Defend China's influence abroad	No	Yes	Yes	No	Yes
Offensive Mission 1: Undermine U.S. and partner legitimacy	Yes	Yes	Yes	No	Yes
Offensive Mission 2: Threaten U.S. partner territory and sovereignty	Yes	Yes	Yes	No	Yes
Offensive Mission 3: Threaten U.S. and partner overseas interests	Yes	Yes	Yes	Yes	Yes
Offensive Mission 4: Undermine U.S. influence abroad	No	Yes	Yes	Yes	No

competition, U.S. actions to exploit Chinese vulnerabilities in a low-intensity conflict invariably carry far greater risks of escalating the conflict. Either way, the U.S. approach could take three broad forms.

First, the United States could seek to deter unwanted PLA actions from occurring by shaping Chinese perceptions of the potential adverse effects of those actions. This approach is particularly applicable to the PLA missions that are likely to create dependencies between China and partner nations that could lead to a protracted conflict, such as missions to defend Chinese interests and influence abroad (Defensive Missions 3 and 4). In a hypothetical low-intensity conflict, the United States could increase pressure on Chinese client states with significant Chinese overseas interests to force CCP decisionmakers to either risk a protracted conflict in that country or abandon their interests entirely—creating strategic openings for the United States to cast China as an unreliable partner.

Alternatively, the United States could exploit the adverse consequences of PLA actions after they occur to limit the CCP's desire to pursue similar efforts through the PLA in the future. The PLA is particularly vulnerable to disruption in its more offensive missions against U.S. partners in a low-intensity conflict (Offensive Missions 1, 2, and 3) in which such activities are likely to generate PLA casualties. The Chinese domestic population's sensitivity to such casualties is likely to create pressure on CCP decisionmakers to limit the PLA's more aggressive unilateral actions, and effective efforts by the United States to amplify these concerns could incentivize the CCP to shift the burden for warfighting onto its limited and less effective foreign proxies. Similarly, the United States could illuminate the economic and societal harm of China's efforts to target U.S. interests and influence abroad in a low-intensity war (Offensive Missions 3 and 4) and exploit China's violation of its oft-stated belief in nonintervention in the internal affairs of foreign countries in the local information environment. The effect could be to disrupt China's ability to gain economic partners down the road and, in the short term as part of a low-intensity conflict, drive more nations to join the United States in an anti-China coalition.

Finally, the United States could exploit specific PLA weaknesses in power projection and partner support to reduce the likelihood of PLA success in any given operation or incentivize CCP decisionmakers to rely on the PLA when other nonmilitary or indirect approaches would be more likely to succeed. This approach is particularly applicable to situations in a low-intensity conflict in which the CCP might task the PLA to carry out demonstrations of combat power to intimidate neighbors and assert its territorial claims (Defensive Mission 2); these demonstrations would be aggressive actions that might be more likely to harden its adversary's resolve than China's current salami-slicing gray-zone tactics. Moreover, potential PLA failures to execute specific military aspects of these demonstrations could be exploited in the information environment to reduce CCP confidence in the ability of the PLA to successfully accomplish those tasks as part of a larger war. Similarly, the United States could leverage potential PLA difficulties in operating abroad in nonpermissive environments or in foreign languages to illuminate evidence of PLA malign activities targeting U.S. and partner interests and influence (Offensive Missions 3 and 4).

CHAPTER 5

Overall Findings and Implications

With the second-largest economy in the world and one of the world's strongest militaries, China poses a formidable military challenge to the United States. Our report considers the ways that the Chinese military could play a significant role both in peacetime competition and in a future scenario in which tensions with the United States have escalated to the level of a low-intensity conflict. In each case, we have analyzed the myriad tasks the PLA could carry out to support the war effort and their associated vulnerabilities to disruption of the successful execution of these tasks.

In this final chapter, we summarize our key findings and conclude with a set of implications for how the United States could seek to frustrate the ability of the CCP to leverage the PLA to achieve its strategic objectives.

The Role of the People's Liberation Army in Peacetime Competition Missions

In peacetime competition with the United States, the PLA's specific roles and tasks would consist of both defensive and offensive tasks. Among defensive tasks in peacetime competition, the PLA would focus heavily on efforts to protect the CCP's rule from potential external threats in competition and Chinese forces would aim to control dangers emanating through cyberspace and the information domain. Deterrence and the protection of sovereignty and territorial claims through whole-of-government methods would remain key responsibilities. China's military could rely on host-nation partner forces and defense contractors to help protect overseas interests, and PLA forces would likely rely on military diplomacy to protect Chinese influence and access around the world.

Among offensive tasks in peacetime competition, the PLA would likely be tasked to counter U.S. influence and erode U.S. military access abroad in competition. Chinese military forces could foment challenges to the rule of key partner governments, notably in Taiwan. Paramilitary forces such as the CCG and PAFMM could contest disputed maritime territory, and Chinese cyber actors could probe vulnerabilities in U.S. overseas military infrastructure. The PLA could also augment diplomats and other government actors to pressure countries into reducing their security commitments with the United States.

The Role of the People's Liberation Army in Low-Intensity Conflict Missions

Beyond peacetime competition tasks, we explored how the dynamics of an escalating rivalry could drive both countries to engage in hostilities against one another. Although many analysts have proposed a major war as the most likely type of conflict, we propose a different path. In our analysis, low-intensity conflict is equally plausible. We explored this possibility through a hypothetical scenario of systemic low-intensity conflict that would span much of the world, involving both defensive and offensive tasks for the PLA to protect Chinese interests and weaken U.S. power in a manner that minimizes the risk of escalation.

Among defensive tasks in low-intensity conflict, the protection of CCP rule would become even more important to the PLA than it is in peacetime. PLA and Chinese security forces could ramp up security to control political opposition, suppress U.S. information operations, and root out U.S. influence in cyberspace. PLA joint forces would prepare for operations to repel any encroachment on Chinese claimed territory by U.S.-backed partner forces, and PLA assets would work with partner militaries and defense contractors to defend overseas assets from potential externally backed sabotage or attack. PLA personnel would also step up military diplomacy, exercises, and training to protect Chinese influence and access.

Among offensive operations in low-intensity conflict, the PLA might carry out its own set of influence and cyber operations to foment unrest in the United States and its key allies, perhaps as a retaliation for intrusions that Beijing ascribed to the United States. Chinese paramilitary and some military forces might be willing to seize contested territory in the first island chain. Chinese saboteurs and cyber units might be more willing to carry out attacks on U.S. military basing infrastructure abroad as part of a low-intensity conflict. Chinese military personnel would augment diplomatic efforts to aggressively undermine U.S. alliances, partnerships, access, and messages.

Implications of the People's Liberation Army's Vulnerabilities to Disruption

Our analysis suggests that the PLA faces many potential vulnerabilities in its ability to support Beijing's broader strategic goals through tasks in peacetime competition and in a low-intensity conflict. We focus specifically on potential CCP concerns about both the unintended effects of PLA actions on domestic instability, escalation risk, and reputational risk and the weaknesses in the PLA's ability to support partners abroad and project power far from the Chinese mainland. These vulnerabilities represent potential pressure points that the United States could exploit to frustrate and shape CCP strategic design in advantageous ways. We identify three broad mechanisms through which the United States could leverage these vulnerabilities to frustrate Beijing's preferred strategies in utilizing the PLA to achieve core strategic objectives.

- **The United States could deter harmful PLA actions** by shaping perceptions of the potential negative effects of those actions to China's own interests.
- **The United States could exploit the adverse consequences of PLA actions** after they occur to deter Beijing from seeking to repeat similar actions.
- **The United States could exploit specific PLA weaknesses** in power projection and partner support to weaken Beijing's confidence in the PLA and discourage similar operations and activities.

Across these various mechanisms, we explore the broader implications for the U.S. military in terms of the potential for strategic disruption of CCP-preferred strategies based on each of the PLA's primary vulnerabilities in peacetime competition and low-intensity conflict. Four implications emerge:

- **Targeting vulnerabilities related to reputational risk of PLA actions.** The predominant vulnerability faced by CCP decisionmakers in employing the PLA to support peacetime competition and low-intensity conflict objectives is the potential for reputational blowback from PLA overreach in conducting both offensive and defensive missions. The United States could illuminate and amplify evidence of PLA coercion and overreach to disrupt China's ability to build partnerships abroad or drive more nations to join in an anti-China coalition as part of a wider low-intensity conflict.
- **Targeting vulnerabilities related to risk of escalation from PLA actions.** Senior CCP decisionmakers will likely face significant concerns about the potential for more-aggressive PLA actions to cause unintended escalation with the United States or its partners or commit China to a protracted conflict or quagmire that threatens its broader development goals. The United States could leverage this vulnerability by increasing pressure on Chinese client states, particularly during a low-intensity conflict, to force CCP decisionmakers to risk protraction if they commit additional resources or risk appearing as an unreliable partner they do not.
- **Targeting vulnerabilities related to domestic instability from PLA actions.** Senior CCP decisionmakers will likely face significant concerns about the potential for specific PLA missions to generate increased domestic instability at home. For obvious reasons, the United States should be careful to avoid escalatory measures that raise CCP concerns about U.S. intentions related to the CCP's legitimacy. However, the United States could look to leverage evidence of the PLA's role in internal security and domestic measures to frustrate Beijing's ability to establish partner relationships abroad. Similarly, the United States could leverage potential Chinese domestic sensitivities to PLA casualties abroad as a way of deterring the CCP from authorizing more-aggressive PLA actions in a low-intensity war.
- **Targeting vulnerabilities related to power projection and partner support.** Vulnerabilities related to the PLA's limited ability to support partners, operate in foreign languages or denied areas, and project power far from the Chinese mainland could also be

exploited by the United States to cast the PLA as an incapable security partner, drive wedges between China and potential partners abroad, and reduce Beijing's confidence in the ability of the PLA to achieve its stated objectives.

People's Liberation Army Missions, Tasks, and Vulnerabilities in Peacetime Competition

This appendix provides a summary of the missions, tasks, and potential vulnerabilities that China's military might undertake in its peacetime competition with the United States. It also lists the forces, method of execution, and potential nonmilitary assets that could be involved in each task.

TABLE A.1

People's Liberation Army Peacetime Competition Missions, Tasks, and Vulnerabilities

PLA Mission	PLA Task	Chinese Forces	Execution	Coordination with Nonmilitary Assets	Potential Vulnerabilities
Defensive Mission 1: Deter and defeat externally backed threats to CCP, basic security, and socialist system	Task 1: Control externally backed threats to ethnic Han dominated areas	• PAP • PLAGF • Militia • PLASSF	• PAP augments law enforcement in suppressing popular challenges to CCP rule • PLA intelligence supports surveillance, monitoring	• Civilian intelligence and security services • CAC • Provincial governments	• Politicization of the PLA as a tool for domestic power • Accelerated domestic unrest and dissatisfaction with the CCP for using the PLA to suppress domestic protests • Potential reputational blowback that damages market access and influence abroad
	Task 2: Control externally backed threats to ethnic minority areas	• PAP • PLAGF • Militia • PLASSF	• PAP augments law enforcement to suppress separatist activity • Counterterrorism operations are conducted • PLA ISR helps monitor separatist groups	• Civilian intelligence and security services • Counterterrorism law enforcement units • CAC • Provincial governments	• Same as above

Table A.1—Continued

PLA Mission	PLA Task	Chinese Forces	Execution	Coordination with Nonmilitary Assets	Potential Vulnerabilities
Defensive Mission 2: Defend China's territory, sovereignty, and national unity from U.S.-backed threats	Task 1: Deter potential U.S. threats to homeland	• PLASSF • PLARF • PLAN • PLAAF • PLA SOF	• PLASSF carries out deterrence and response operations against potential nuclear, conventional, cyber, and space threats	• Civilian intelligence and security services • UFWD	• Risk of unintended escalation that stymies decisionmaking • Potential reputational backlash and aggravated threat perceptions from aggressive measures to protect Chinese sovereignty claims • Unknown adequacy of PLA forces and execution of military operations
	Task 2: Deter potential externally backed threats to China's sovereign territory	• PLA (all services)	• PLA patrols border regions and ensures readiness to defeat any incursion or attack on maritime and land borders	• Civilian intelligence and security services • Provincial governments • MFA • UFWD	• Same as above
	Task 3: Deter Taiwan from externally backed separatist activity	• PLA (all services)	• PLA maintains readiness to defeat any externally backed separatist activity, demonstrates combat power, coerces Taiwan	• TAO • Civilian intelligence and security services • UFWD	• Same as above

Table A.1—Continued

PLA Mission	PLA Task	Chinese Forces	Execution	Coordination with Nonmilitary Assets	Potential Vulnerabilities
Defensive Mission 3: Defend Chinese overseas interests from U.S.-backed threats	Task 1: Deter externally backed threats against overseas assets, citizens	• PLA (all services)	• PLA operations are conducted where feasible to control threats • Coordinate with PSCs and host-nation militaries as needed to protect Chinese assets	• MFA • PMC • Host-nation militaries and security forces	• Inadequate power projection capabilities • Limited ability and experience assisting partner states with security needs and potential reputational damage from failure to do so • Aggravated threat perceptions in response to Chinese coercion • Domestic sensitivity to PLA casualties
	Task 2: Provide military assistance to protect client state assets, citizens from externally backed threats	• PMC • PLA technicians and advisers	• Conduct intelligence-sharing, combined exercises, joint patrols, arms sales to help partner control threats	• MFA • PMC • Host-nation militaries and security forces	• Same as above
Defensive Mission 4: Defend China's influence, access, partnerships, and narrative from U.S. subversion attempts	Task 1: Counter U.S. efforts to undermine China's influence, access, and partnerships	• PLA (all services) • PAP	• PLA officials pressure host nations to downgrade U.S. access, influence as a condition for Chinese benefits	• MFA • UFWD • Propaganda-media	• Limited impact of military diplomacy or information operations on broader efforts to promote to political, economic relationships • Limited experience working with foreign partners and limited appeal compared with U.S. security partnerships
	Task 2: Counter U.S. efforts to undermine China's global narrative	• PLASSF	• PLA specialists support civilian propaganda, messaging	• MFA • UFWD • Propaganda-media	• Same as above

PLA Mission	PLA Task	Chinese Forces	Execution	Coordination with Nonmilitary Assets	Potential Vulnerabilities
Offensive Mission 1: Undermine and threaten government, basic security, and social stability of the United States and its allies	Task 1: Prepare options to threaten the legitimacy and social stability of the United States and its key Asian allies and partners	• PLASSF • PLA SOF	• PLASSF units identify vulnerabilities in enemy cyber networks, information domains that can be targeted in wartime	• Civilian intelligence and security services • UFWD	• Disclosure of Chinese government involvement that damages China's reputation and influence
Offensive Mission 2: Support threats to the territory and sovereignty of U.S. allies	Task 1: Support authorities in consolidating control over disputed areas occupied by U.S. allies and partners	• PLA (all services) • PLASSF • CCG • Militia	• PLA forces carry out patrols, ensure readiness, and coordinate operations with nonmilitary assets for gray-zone operations	• MFA • Propaganda-media • Civilian intelligence and security services • State Council • Provincial governments	• Aggressive measures to consolidate control creating instability on China's borders • Aggressive measures hardening adversary resolve
Offensive Mission 3: Support threats to overseas interests of the United States and its allies	Task 1: Prepare options to militarily damage United States and its allied overseas interests	• PLASSF • PLA SOF	• PLA works with civilian intelligence to develop accesses, recruit agents, carry out reconnaissance	• Civilian intelligence	• Difficulty in accessing U.S., allied networks, facilities • Disclosure of efforts to develop options fueling tensions and damaging China's reputation • Limited overseas posture and partner relationships
Offensive Mission 4: Undermine U.S. influence, access, alliances, partnerships, and narrative	Task 1: Erode and undermine U.S. military influence, access, and partnerships	• PLA (all services) • PAP	• PLA officials pressure host nations to downgrade U.S. access, influence for Chinese benefits	• MFA • Propaganda-media • UFWD	• Chinese efforts to undermine alliances backfiring and weakening China's reputation and influence
	Task 2: Erode and undermine U.S. global narrative on security topics	• PLASSF	• PLA specialists support civilian propaganda, messaging	• MFA • Propaganda-media • UFWD	• Same as above

People's Liberation Army Missions, Tasks, and Potential Vulnerabilities in Low-Intensity Conflict

This appendix provides a summary of the missions, tasks, and potential vulnerabilities that China's military might undertake in a hypothetical low-intensity conflict with the United States. It also lists the forces, method of execution, and potential nonmilitary assets that could be involved in each task.

TABLE B.1

People's Liberation Army Low-Intensity Conflict Missions, Tasks, and Vulnerabilities

PLA Mission	PLA Tasks	Chinese Forces	Execution	Coordination with Nonmilitary Assets	Potential Vulnerabilities
Defensive Mission 1: Deter and defeat externally backed threats to CCP, basic security, and socialist system	Task 1: Deter externally backed conventional, space, cyber, and nuclear strikes	• PAP • PLA (all services)	• PLA cyber units support domestic law enforcement to protect cyber infrastructure; PLA intelligence helps monitor foreign threats to space, domestic infrastructure • PAP patrols and guards facilities • PLARF carries out deterrence missions	• Civilian intelligence and security services • Militia • MFA, propaganda-media, CAC	• Difficulties of securing soft targets • Burden of heavy security could impair economy • Domestic discontent growing from heavy repression
	Task 2: Control threats to CCP rule in Han-dominant and ethnic-minority regions	• PAP • PLAGF • Militia	• PAP and PLA forces augment law enforcement in monitoring and suppressing popular protests, demonstrations, and other potential externally backed domestic challenges to CCP rule • PAP and PLA forces capture any foreign agents fomenting unrest	• Civilian intelligence and security service • UFWD • CAC	• Same as above
	Task 3: Deter and defeat enemy efforts to undermine CCP rule through information operations	• PLASSF • Joint Staff Department's Information and Communications Bureau	• PLASSF carries out reconnaissance of enemy cyber forces, operations to counter U.S.-disinformation and other information operations	• Propaganda-media • Civilian intelligence and security services • CAC	• Same as above

Table B.1—Continued

PLA Mission	PLA Tasks	Chinese Forces	Execution	Coordination with Nonmilitary Assets	Potential Vulnerabilities
Defensive Mission 2: Deter and defeat externally backed threats to China's territory, sovereignty, and national unity	Task 1: Deter and defeat incursions into land and maritime border areas by externally backed adversaries	• PLA (all services) • PLASSF • CCG • Militia	• Joint forces carry out combat operations to drive any forces that invade Chinese territory out while controlling escalation	• Civilian intelligence and security services • UFWD • MFA • State Council • Provincial governments	• Unknown adequacy of PLA forces and execution of military operations • Risk of escalation and economic damage from aggressive measures to protect Chinese sovereignty claims • Hardened adversary popular resolve to resist Chinese coercion • Reputational blowback in fence-sitting countries
	Task 2: Defeat separatist threats in Western provinces	• PAP • PLASSF • PLAGF	• PAP augments law enforcement in suppressing large-scale riots, counterterrorism operations, and patrolling minority regions • PLA supports security as necessary and helps locate and neutralize foreign agents	• Civilian intelligence and security services, UFWD, MFA	• Same as above
	Task 3: Defend and defeat Taiwan separatist movements	• PLA (all services), • CCG • Militia	• PLA joint force carries out deterrence operations, conducts coercive gray-zone actions to prevent Taiwan independence	• Civilian intelligence and security services • UFWD • State Council • TAO	• Same as above

Table B.1—Continued

PLA Mission	PLA Tasks	Chinese Forces	Execution	Coordination with Nonmilitary Assets	Potential Vulnerabilities
Defensive Mission 3: Deter and defeat externally backed threats to Chinese overseas interests	Task 1: Degrade or destroy potential externally backed nonstate actor or proxy threats	• PLA (all services) • PLA SOF • PLA techs • PLASS • PAP	• PLA technicians support arms sales and joint patrols with host nation • PAP supports counterterrorism operations with host-nation law enforcement • PLA joint operations against nonstate actors in border areas	• MFA • Host-nation intelligence and security forces • PSC	• Limited power projection capabilities likely to be stressed in wartime • Heavy reliance on partners with limited warfighting capabilities creating potential dependencies • Limited ability to defend against physical vulnerabilities to key infrastructure abroad • Potential for popular backlash and violence against Chinese presence or coercion
	Task 2: Protect key infrastructure from sabotage or attack from foreign agents or armed groups	• PAP • PLAGF • PLA SOF • PLANMC	• PAP patrol areas near critical infrastructure • Local forces cooperate with PLA to protect assets • PLA prepares for NEO of Chinese civilians	• MFA • PSCs • Host-nation intelligence and security forces	• Same as above

Table B.1—Continued

PLA Mission	PLA Tasks	Chinese Forces	Execution	Coordination with Nonmilitary Assets	Potential Vulnerabilities
Defensive Mission 4: Defend China's influence, access, partnerships, and narrative from U.S. subversion attempts	Task 1: Defeat U.S. efforts to subvert military partnerships	• PLA (all services) • PAP • CCG	• Identify and counter U.S. influence operations through intelligence, military diplomacy, joint exercises, and engagements	• Host-nation military • SOEs (for military equipment and finance • MFA • Embassies • UFWD • Civilian intelligence	• Lack of power projection capabilities • Risk of protracted involvement in supporting besieged partner nation • Risk of popular backlash from coercion to shore up political pressure • Risk of escalation that drives greater U.S. military involvement
	Task 2: Support client military in proxy wars against U.S.-backed partner	• PLA (all services) • PAP	• Provide arms, training, intelligence, joint combat operations support, long-range tactical or strategic strikes, or support counterinsurgency operations	• Host-nation military • MFA • Embassies • UFWD • Civilian intelligence	• Same as above

Table B.1—Continued

PLA Mission	PLA Tasks	Chinese Forces	Execution	Coordination with Nonmilitary Assets	Potential Vulnerabilities
Offensive Mission 1: Undermine and threaten government, basic security, and social system of the United States and its allies	Task 1. Prepare continental U.S. cyberstrike options	• PLASSF • PLA intelligence, • PLAR • PLAN • PLAAF	• Develop target sets, develop accesses to networks and facilities • Deploy surveillance hardware • Recruit U.S.-based agents	• UFWD • Civilian intelligence and security service • MFA	• Risk of social and economic harm from tit-for-tat escalation • Limited ability to operate in nonpermissive environments • Risk of backlash from intrusive Chinese interference in domestic politics
	Task 2. Conduct subversion and foment domestic unrest in United States and its allied countries	• PLASSF • PLA SOF	• Provide arms, supplies, and funds for opposition groups through information operations, clandestine operations • Execute disinformation campaigns, sabotage, covert operations	• UFWD • Civilian intelligence and security service • MFA	• Same as above
Offensive Mission 2: Threaten the territory and sovereignty of U.S. allies	Task 1: PLA directly challenges or supports partner who contends for territory in U.S.-backed partner states	• PLA (all services) • PLA intelligence • CCG • PLASSF	• PLA conducts joint operations to contest territory • Arms sales, technical assistance, ISR, and PLA SOF support are provided to client militaries fighting U.S.-backed partners over territory	• MFA • Embassies • UFWD • Partner-nation military force • PMC • Civilian intelligence	• Escalation risks from supporting threats to sovereignty of territory controlled by other countries and ensuing instability • Risks to PLA forces conducting operations abroad and sensitivity at home to PLA casualties • Danger of reputational damage from aggressive actions

Table B.1—Continued

PLA Mission	PLA Tasks	Chinese Forces	Execution	Coordination with Nonmilitary Assets	Potential Vulnerabilities
Offensive Mission 3: Threaten overseas interests of the United States and its allies	Task 1: Damage externally backed partner country infrastructure, assets	• PLA SOF • PLASSF	• Carry out clandestine sabotage of key infrastructure targets • Carry out cyberattacks on infrastructure	• MFA • Civilian intelligence • MSS • Partner countries	• Limited ability to operate in denied environments or project power • Risk of retaliatory strikes against Chinese infrastructure • Reputational blowback on China in affected countries
Offensive Mission 4: Undermine U.S. influence, access, alliances, partnerships, and narrative	Task 1: Erode U.S. military influence, alliances and partnerships, and access	• PLASSF • PLA intelligence agencies • PLA SOF	• Conduct military diplomacy, disinformation campaigns, identification and funding of local political proxies, exfiltration and leaking of information, identification and harassment of spreaders of counternarratives, and military intimidation	• MFA • UFWD • Civilian security and intelligence • Propaganda-media	• Escalation risk inviting direct intervention by U.S. forces or protraction of conflict • Risk of reputational damage and reduced influence • Limited ability to operate through partners in nonpermissive environments or in foreign languages
	Task 2: Erode confidence in U.S. power through military demonstrations	• PLAN • PLAAF • PLARF • PLAGF • PLA publicity organs	• Major naval exercises, including amphibious exercises • Weapon tests, demonstrations of military might	• MFA • UFWD • Civilian security and intelligence • Propaganda-media	• Same as above
	Task 3: Support overthrow of U.S.-backed regimes (as needed)	• PLAGF • PLA SOF • PLA intelligence bodies	• Clandestinely distribute arms, supplies, and funds • Set up and staff training camps • Provide battlefield intelligence • PLA potentially invades	• MSS • UFWD • Civilian security and intelligence	• Same as above

Abbreviations

BRI	Belt and Road Initiative
CAC	Cyberspace Administration of China
CCG	Chinese Coast Guard
CCP	Chinese Communist Party
DIME	diplomatic, informational, military, or economic
ISR	intelligence, surveillance, and reconnaissance
MFA	Ministry of Foreign Affairs
MSS	Ministry of State Security
PAP	People's Armed Police
PAFM	People's Armed Forces Militia
PAFMM	People's Armed Forces Maritime Militia
PLA	People's Liberation Army
PLAAF	People's Liberation Army Air Force
PLAGF	People's Liberation Army Ground Force
PLAJLSF	People's Liberation Army Joint Logistics Support Force
PLAN	People's Liberation Army Navy
PLANMC	People's Liberation Army Navy Marine Corps
PLARF	People's Liberation Army Rocket Force
PLASSF	People's Liberation Army Strategic Support Force
PLA SOF	People's Liberation Army Special Operations Force
PSC	private security company
SOE	state-owned enterprise
TAO	Taiwan Affairs Office
UFWD	United Front Work Department

References

Unless otherwise indicated, the authors of this report provided the translations of bibliographic details for the non-English sources included in this report. To support conventions for alphabetizing, sources in Chinese are introduced with and organized according to their English translations. The original rendering in Chinese appears in brackets after the English translation.

Akil, Samy, and Karam Shaar, *The Red Dragon in the Land of Jasmine: An Overview of China's Role in the Syrian Conflict*, Operations and Policy Center, March 24, 2021.

Allen, Kenneth, Philip C. Saunders, and John Chen, *Chinese Military Diplomacy 2003–2016: Trends and Implications*, National Defense University Press, 2017.

Anand, Dibyesh, "Colonization with Chinese Characteristics: Politics of (In)security in Xinjiang and Tibet," *Asian Survey*, Vol. 38, No. 1, 2019.

Arduino, Alessandro, "China's Private Security Companies: The Evolution of a New Security Actor," in Nadège Rolland, ed., *Securing the Belt and Road Initiative: China's Evolving Military Engagement Along the Silk Roads*, National Bureau of Asian Research, September 3, 2019.

Barnett, Robert, "China Is Building Entire Villages in Another Country's Territory," *Foreign Policy*, May 7, 2021.

Beauchamp-Mustafaga, Nathan, "Cognitive Domain Operations," *China Brief*, Vol. 19, No. 16, September 6, 2019.

Beauchamp-Mustafaga, Nathan, "Where to Next? PLA Considerations for Overseas Base Selection," *China Brief*, Vol. 20, No. 18, October 19, 2020.

Blinken, Antony J., "The Administration's Approach to the People's Republic of China," speech delivered at George Washington University, Asia Society, May 26, 2022.

Boston University Global Development Policy Center, "China's Overseas Development Finance Database," last updated January 23, 2023. As of April 18, 2023: https://www.bu.edu/gdp/chinas-overseas-development-finance/

Brady, Anne-Marie, "New Zealand's Quiet China Shift," *The Diplomat*, July 2020.

Branigan, Tania, "China Lambasts U.S. over South China Sea Row," *The Guardian*, August 6, 2012.

Brecher, Michael, "Crisis, Conflict, War: The State of the Discipline," *International Political Science Review*, Vol. 17, No. 2, April 1996.

Brook, Timothy, *Quelling the People: The Military Suppression of the Beijing Democracy Movement*, Oxford University Press, 1992.

Brooker, Matthew, "'Red Roulette' Uncovers Covert Hands in Hong Kong," Bloomberg, October 3, 2021.

Chang, Joshua, "China's Arms Diplomacy in Venezuela Affects Stability in the Western Hemisphere," *Georgetown Security Studies Review*, October 27, 2020.

Chin, Josh, "China Spends More on Domestic Security as Xi's Powers Grow," *Wall Street Journal*, March 6, 2018.

"China Must Be Ready for Worsened North Korea Ties," *Global Times*, April 27, 2017.

China Power Team, "How Is China Bolstering Its Military Diplomatic Relations?" ChinaPower, Center for Strategic and International Studies, August 26, 2020.

"China to Defend Fairness and Justice in the Multilateral Arena: FM," Xinhua, December 30, 2021.

"China, U.S. Stand to Gain from Cooperation, Lose from Confrontation: Foreign Minister," Xinhua, March 8, 2019.

"China's International Development Cooperation in the New Era," Xinhua, January 10, 2021.

"Chinese Envoy Urges Formulating International Rules for Cyberspace Generally Accepted by All Nations," Xinhua, June 30, 2021.

"Chinese Groups Seen Forging Ties with Okinawa Independence Activists," *Japan Times*, December 27, 2016.

Clark, Bryan, Timothy A. Walton, Melinda Tourangeau, and Steve Tourangeau, *The Invisible Battlefield: A Technology Strategy for U.S. Electromagnetic Spectrum Superiority*, Hudson Institute, March 10, 2021.

"Commentary: China, U.S. Can 'Cooperate' to Make Bigger Pie for Lunch," Xinhua, May 6, 2019.

Cordesman, Anthony H., and Joseph Kendall, *Chinese Strategy and Military Modernization in 2016*, Center for Strategic and International Studies, December 2016.

Costello, John, and Joe McReynolds, "China's Strategic Support Force: A Force for a New Era," in Philip C. Saunders, Arthur S. Ding, Andrew Scobell, Andrew N. D. Yang, and Joel Wuthnow, eds., *Chairman Xi Remakes the PLA: Assessing Chinese Military Reforms*, National Defense University Press, 2019.

Cuenca, Oliver, "Ethiopia-Djibouti Line Reports Reduced Revenue Due to Vandalism," *International Railway Journal*, December 16, 2020.

Dobbins, James, Andrew Scobell, Edmund J. Burke, David C. Gompert, Derek Grossman, Eric Heginbotham, and Howard J. Shatz, *Conflict with China Revisited: Prospects, Consequences, and Strategies for Deterrence*, RAND Corporation, PE-248-A, 2017. As of April 17, 2023: https://www.rand.org/pubs/perspectives/PE248.html

Dou, Eva, "What Is—and Isn't—in the Joint Statement from Putin and Xi," *Washington Post*, February 4, 2022.

Duan Junze [段君泽], "Russian 'Hybrid Warfare' Application and Its Influence" [俄式 "混合战争" 实践及其影响], *Modern International Relations* [现代国际关系], Vol. 3, 2017.

Efron, Shira, Kurt Klein, and Raphael S. Cohen, *Environment, Geography, and the Future of Warfare: The Changing Global Environment and its Implications for the U.S. Air Force*, RAND Corporation, RR-2849/5-AF, 2020. As of April 17, 2023: https://www.rand.org/pubs/research_reports/RR2849z5.html

Erickson, Andrew, and Austin Strange, *No Substitute for Experience: Chinese Anti-Piracy Operations in the Gulf of Aden*, Naval War College, November 2013.

Erwin, Sandra, "Pentagon Report: China Amassing Arsenal of Anti-Satellite Weapons," *SpaceNews*, September 1, 2020.

Fedasiuk, Ryan, "Buying Silence: The Price of Internet Censorship in China," *China Brief*, Vol. 21, No. 1, January 12, 2021.

Feng, Emily, "'Afraid We Will Become the Next Xinjiang': China's Hui Muslims Face Crackdown," NPR, September 26, 2019.

Feng, Emily, "China Makes It a Crime to Question Military Casualties on the Internet," NPR, March 22, 2021.

Feng, John, "Taiwan's Desire for Unification with China Near Record Low as Tensions Rise," *Newsweek*, July 14, 2022.

Fravel, M. Taylor, *China's Military Strategy Since 1949: Active Defense*, Princeton University Press, 2019.

Freymann, Eyck, "Influence Without Entanglement in the Middle East," *Foreign Policy*, February 25, 2021.

Fu Ying, "The US World Order Is a Suit That No Longer Fits," *Financial Times*, January 6, 2016.

"Full Text of Xi Jinping's Report at 19th CPC National Congress," Xinhua, November 3, 2017.

Gaddis, John, *The Cold War: A New History*, Penguin Books, 2005.

Gettleman, Jeffrey, "Anger Surges in India over Deadly Border Brawl with China," *New York Times*, June 18, 2020.

Gettleman, Jeffrey, Emily Schmall, and Hari Kumar, "New India-China Border Clash Shows Simmering Tensions," *New York Times*, September 24, 2021.

Gompert, David C., Astrid Stuth Cevallos, and Cristina L. Garafola, *War with China: Thinking Through the Unthinkable*, RAND Corporation, RR-1140-A, 2016. As of April 17, 2023: https://www.rand.org/pubs/research_reports/RR1140.html

Graceffo, Antonio, "China's Crackdown on Mongolian Culture," *The Diplomat*, September 4, 2020.

Greitens, Sheena Chestnut, *Dealing with Demand for China's Global Surveillance Exports*, Brookings Institution, April 2020.

Harold, Scott W., Nathan Beauchamp-Mustafaga, and Jeffrey W. Hornung, *Chinese Disinformation Efforts on Social Media*, RAND Corporation, RR-4373/3-AF, 2021. As of April 17, 2023: https://www.rand.org/pubs/research_reports/RR4373z3.html

Heath, Timothy R., Christian Curriden, Bryan Frederick, Nathan Chandler, and Jennifer Kavanagh, *China's Military Interventions: Patterns, Drivers, and Signposts*, RAND Corporation, RR-A444-4, 2021. As of April 17, 2023: https://www.rand.org/pubs/research_reports/RRA444-4.html

Heath, Timothy R., Derek Grossman, and Asha Clark, *China's Quest for Global Primacy: An Analysis of Chinese International and Defense Strategies to Outcompete the United States*, RAND Corporation, RR-A447-1, 2021. As of April 17, 2023: https://www.rand.org/pubs/research_reports/RRA447-1.html

Heath, Timothy R., Kristen Gunness, and Tristan Finazzo, *The Return of Great Power War: Scenarios of Systemic Conflict Between the United States and China*, RAND Corporation, RR-A830-1, 2022. As of April 17, 2023: https://www.rand.org/pubs/research_reports/RRA830-1.html

Heath, Timothy R., and Matthew Lane, *Science Based Scenario Design: A Proposed Method to Support Political-Strategic Analysis*, RAND Corporation, RR-2833-OSD, 2019. As of May 18, 2023: https://www.rand.org/pubs/research_reports/RR2833.html

Heginbotham, Eric, Michael Nixon, Forrest Morgan, Jacob Heim, Jeff Hagan, Sheng Li, Jeffrey Engstrom, Martin Libicki, Paul DeLuca, David Shlapak, David Frelinger, Burgess Laird, Kyle Brady, and Lyle Morris, *The U.S. China Military Scorecard: Forces, Geography, and the Evolving Balance of Power 1996–2017*, RAND Corporation, RR-392-AF, 2015. As of April 17, 2023: https://www.rand.org/pubs/research_reports/RR392.html

Heim, Jacob L., and Benjamin M. Miller, *Measuring Power, Power Cycles, and the Risk of Great-Power War in the 21st Century*, RAND Corporation, RR-2989, 2020. As of April 17, 2023: https://www.rand.org/pubs/research_reports/RR2989.html

Henderson, Scott, "Polyglot Dragon," *Armed Forces Journal*, Vol. 149, No. 1, November 2011.

Herlevi, April, "China as a Niche Arms Exporter," Centers for Naval Analysis, August 31, 2021.

Higgins, Andrew, "China's Theory for Hong Kong Protests: Secret American Meddling," *New York Times*, August 8, 2019.

Hille, Kathrin, and Demetri Sevastopulo, "Chinese Warplanes Simulated Attacking U.S. Carrier Near Taiwan," *Financial Times*, January 29, 2021.

Hillman, Jennifer, and Alex Tippett, "Who Built That? Labor and the Belt and Road Initiative," *The Internationalist*, blog, Council for Foreign Relations, July 6, 2021.

Hoo Tiang Boon, "Xi-Biden Summit: Finding the Contours of Responsible Competition," *Straits Times*, November 18, 2021.

Huang Linhao [黄林昊], "Chinese Representative Calls for the Creation of a Digital Database to Prevent the Cross-Border Flow of Terrorists" [中国代表呼吁尽快建立数据库遏制恐怖分子跨国流动], *People's Daily* [人民日报], June 17, 2015.

Huang, Joyce, "China Using 'Cognitive Warfare' Against Taiwan, Observers Say," *Voice of America,* January 17, 2021.

Huang, Kristin, "Chinese Military Drills Simulate Amphibious Landing and Island Seizure in Battle Conditions," *South China Morning Post*, July 28, 2021.

Human Rights Watch, *"I Saw It With My Own Eyes": Abuses by Chinese Security Forces in Tibet, 2008–2010*, July 21, 2010.

Human Rights Watch, *"Break Their Lineages, Break Their Roots": China's Crimes Against Humanity Targeting Uyghurs and Other Turkic Muslims*, April 19, 2021.

Hussein, Mohammed, and Mohammed Haddad, "Infographic: US Military Presence Around the World," *Al Jazeera*, September 10, 2021.

"India-China Clash: 20 Indian Troops Killed in Ladakh Fighting," BBC News, June 16, 2020.

International Crisis Group, *Disorder on the Border: Keeping the Peace Between Colombia and Venezuela*, December 14, 2020.

Ip, Cyril, "Chinese PLA Drills Simulating Taiwan Blockade Seen to Become New 'Normal,'" *South China Morning Post*, August 9, 2022.

Islamabad, S. Khan, "Can Pakistan Secure Chinese Investment in Balochistan?" Deutsche Welle, July 14, 2021.

Janes, "Army of Autonomy: The Rise of the United Wa State Army," *Jane's Defense Weekly*, January 8, 2016.

Janes, "United Wa State Army," *Jane's World Insurgency and Terrorism*, May 16, 2019.

Jennings, Ralph, "What Does China's New Land Borders Law Mean for Its Neighbors?," *Voice of America*, November 5, 2021.

Jingdong Yuan, "China's Private Security Contractors and the Protection of Chinese Economic Interests Abroad," *Small Wars and Insurgencies*, Vol. 33, No. 1, 2022.

Kalita, Prabin, "Ulfa-I Operating from Base in China: Centre Tells Tribunal," *Times of India*, October 4, 2020.

Keaten, Jamey, "China's Xi Rejects 'Cold War Mentality,' Pushes Cooperation," Associated Press, January 17, 2022.

Kelion, Leo, "Huawei 5G Kit Must be Removed from U.K. by 2027," BBC News, July 14, 2020.

Khan, Wajahat, and Ken Moriyasu, "U.S. Arms Sales in Indo-Pacific Pick Up as China Tensions Build," *Nikkei Asia*, August 21, 2020.

Kuo, Lily, "Taiwan Election: Tsai Ing-Wen Wins Landslide in Rebuke to China," *The Guardian*, January 11, 2020.

Kurlantzick, Joshua, "How China Is Interfering in Taiwan's Election," Council on Foreign Relations, November 7, 2019.

Kurlantzick, Joshua, "China's Already Poor Global Image Is Being Hurt by Ukraine War," *Asia Unbound*, blog, Council for Foreign Relations, March 24, 2022.

Langeland, Krista, and Derek Grossman, *Tailoring Deterrence for China in Space*, RAND Corporation, RR-A943-1, 2021. As of April 17, 2023:
https://www.rand.org/pubs/research_reports/RRA943-1.html

Legarda, Helena, and Meia Nouwens, *Guardians of the Belt and Road: The Internationalization of China's Private Security Companies*, Mercator Institute for China Studies, August 16, 2018.

Li, Cheng, and Lucy Xu, "Chinese Enthusiasm and American Cynicism over the 'New Type of Great Power Relations,'" *Brookings Institution*, December 4, 2014.

Liu Kun [刘昆], "Should We Take America's Gun? An Analysis of Chinese Military Interference in Iraq" [接过美国的枪? 中国武力干涉伊拉克前景分析], *Global Times* [环球], June 19, 2014.

Liu Wei [刘伟], "Building a City's Anti-Air Efforts into a Modern 'Iron Fortress'" [打造现代城市防空的"铜墙铁壁"], *China Defense* [中国国防报], May 15, 2019.

Liu Xin, "U.S. Escalates Containment of China by Targeting China's Influence on UN: Analyst," *Global Times*, June 17, 2021.

Liu Xuanzun, "PLA Prepared as U.S., Secessionists Provoke," *Global Times*, April 8, 2021.

Luo Shuxian and Jonathan G. Panter, "China's Maritime Militia and Fishing Fleets," *Military Review*, January-February 2021.

Markusen, Max, "A Stealth Industry: The Quiet Expansion of Chinese Private Security Companies," Center for Strategic and International Studies, January 12, 2022.

Mattis, Peter, "China's 'Three Warfares' in Perspective," *War on the Rocks*, January 30, 2018.

Mazarr, Michael J., Samuel Charap, Abigail Casey, Irina A. Chindea, Christian Curriden, Alyssa Demus, Bryan Frederick, Arthur Chan, John P. Godges, Eugeniu Han, Timothy R. Heath, Logan Ma, Elina Treyger, Teddy Ulin, and Ali Wyne, *Stabilizing Great-Power Rivalries*, RAND Corporation, RR-A456-1, 2021. As of April 18, 2023:
https://www.rand.org/pubs/research_reports/RRA456-1.html

Mehta, Aaron, "Two U.S. Airmen Injured by Chinese Lasers Near Djibouti, DoD Says," *Defense News*, May 3, 2018.

Meick, Ethan, and Nargiza Salidjanova, *China's Response to U.S.-South Korea Missile Defense System Deployment and Its Implications*, U.S. China Economic and Security Review Commission, July 2017.

"More Countries Criticize China at UN for Repression of Uighurs," *Al Jazeera*, October 22, 2021.

Morris, Lyle J., Michael J. Mazarr, Jeffrey W. Hornung, Stephanie Pezard, Anika Binnendijk, and Marta Kepe, *Gaining Competitive Advantage in the Gray Zone: Response Options for Coercive Aggression Below the Threshold of Major War*, Santa Monica, Calif., RR-2942-OSD, 2019. As of April 18, 2023:
https://www.rand.org/pubs/research_reports/RR2942.html

Myers, Steven Lee, "In Hong Kong Protests, China Angrily Connects Dots Back to U.S.," *New York Times*, November 30, 2020.

Myers, Steven Lee, "China Bolsters Its Nuclear Options with New Missile Silos in a Desert," *New York Times*, November 3, 2021.

"National Security Office of Central Government Says U.S. Plotting to Wage 'Color Revolution' in Hong Kong," Xinhua, September 25, 2021.

Nelsen, Harvey, "Military Forces in the Cultural Revolution," *China Quarterly*, Vol. 51, July 1972.

Office of the Secretary of Defense, *Military and Security Developments Regarding the People's Republic of China 2021*, U.S. Department of Defense, November 3, 2021.

Ordoñez, Franco, "U.S., China Accuse Each Other of Mishandling COVID-19," NPR, March 23, 2020.

Parakilas, Jacob, "The China-US Arms Trade Arms Race," *The Diplomat*, August 6, 2021.

Poling, Gregory B., Harrison Prétat, and Tabitha Grace Mallory, *Pulling Back the Curtain on China's Maritime Militia*, Center for Strategic and International Studies, November 18, 2021.

Pollpeter, Kevin L., Michael S. Chase, and Eric Heginbotham, *The Creation of the PLA Strategic Support Force and Its Implications for Chinese Military Space Operations*, RAND Corporation, RR-2058-AF, 2017. As of April 18, 2023:
https://www.rand.org/pubs/research_reports/RR2058.html

Rippa, Alessandro, and Martin Saxer, "Mong La: Business as Usual in the China-Myanmar Borderlands," *Cross-Currents: East Asian History and Culture Review*, No. 19, June 2016.

Robinson, Eric, Timothy R. Heath, Gabrielle Tarini, Daniel Egel, Mace Moesner, Christian Curriden, Derek Grossman, and Sale Lilly, *Strategic Disruption by Special Operations Forces: A Concept for Proactive Campaigning Short of Traditional War*, RAND Corporation, RR-A1794-1, 2023.

Rolland, Nadège, ed., *Securing the Belt and Road Initiative: China's Evolving Military Engagement Along the Silk Roads*, National Bureau of Asian Research, September 3, 2019.

"Russia, China Oppose Color Revolutions—Joint Statement," TASS, February 4, 2022.

Saunders, Philip C., and Joel Wuthnow, "Large and In Charge: Civil-Military Relations Under Xi Jinping," in Philip C. Saunders, Arthur S. Ding, Andrew Scobell, Andrew N. D. Yang, and Joel Wuthnow, eds., *Chairman Xi Remakes the PLA: Assessing Chinese Military Reforms*, National Defense University Press, 2019.

Scobell, Andrew, Edmund J. Burke, Cortez A. Cooper III, Sale Lilly, Chad J. R. Ohlandt, Eric Warner, and J. D. Williams, *China's Grand Strategy*, RAND Corporation, RR-2798-A, 2020. As of April 18, 2023:
https://www.rand.org/pubs/research_reports/RR2798.html

Searight, Amy, "Countering China's Influence Operations: Lessons from Australia," Center for Strategic and International Studies, May 8, 2020.

Segal, Adam, *China's Vision for Cyber Sovereignty and the Global Governance of Cyberspace*, National Bureau of Asian Research, August 25, 2020.

Shih, Gerry, "In Central Asia's Forbidding Highlands, a Quiet Newcomer: Chinese Troops," *Washington Post*, February 18, 2019.

Silver, Laura, Kat Devlin, and Christine Huang, "Unfavorable Views of China Reach Historic Highs in Many Countries," Pew Research Center, October 6, 2020.

State Council Information Office, *China's Military Strategy*, May 2015.

State Council Information Office, *China's Policies on Asia-Pacific Security Cooperation*, January 2017.

State Council Information Office, *China's National Defense in the New Era*, July 24, 2019.

State Council Information Office, "Regulations for the Protection of Critical Information Infrastructure [关键信息基础设施安全保护条例]," July 30, 2021.

"Strengthening Taiwan's Resistance," editorial, *Wall Street Journal*, July 22, 2021.

Takagi, Koichiro, "The Future of China's Cognitive Domain Operations: Lessons from the War in Ukraine," *War on the Rocks*, July 22, 2022.

"Thirty Chinese Military Aircraft Enter Taiwan ADIZ," *Focus Taiwan*, May 30, 2022.

Tiezzi, Shannon, "Chinese Nationals Evacuate Yemen on PLA Navy Frigate," *The Diplomat*, March 30, 2015.

"U.S. Adds 14 Chinese Companies to Economic Blacklist Over Xinjiang," Reuters, July 10, 2021.

U.S. Central Intelligence Agency, *The World Factbook*, 2022.

U.S. Department of Defense, *2022 National Defense Strategy of the United States of America*, October 27, 2022.

van Tol, Jan, Mark Gunzinger, Andrew F. Krepinevich, and Jim Thomas, *Air Sea Battle: A Point of Departure Concept*, Center for Strategic and Budgetary Assessments, 2010.

Wang, Chenyi, "The Chinese Communist Party's Relationship with the Khmer Rouge in the 1970s: An Ideological Victory and a Strategic Failure," working paper, Wilson Center, December 2018.

Wang Hongyi [王洪一], "The Influence of New Security Challenges in Africa on Sino-African Cooperation" [非洲安全新挑战及其对中非合作的影响], China Institute of International Studies [中国国际问题研究院], July 25, 2018.

Wang Xiangsui [王湘穗], "Analysis of Future Hybrid Warfare" [未来混合战争形式解析], *Military Digest* [军事文摘], 2021.

Weitz, Richard, "Assessing Chinese-Russian Military Exercises: Past Progress and Future Trends," Center for Strategic and International Studies, July 2021.

White House, *National Security Strategy of the United States of America*, December 18, 2017.

"Who Are the Uyghurs and Why Is China Being Accused of Genocide?" BBC News, June 21, 2021.

Wong, Edward, "Solomon Islands Suspends Visits by Foreign Military Ships, Raising Concerns in U.S.," *New York Times*, August 30, 2022.

Wu, Debby, "China Targets Corporate Backers of Taiwan's Ruling Party," Bloomberg, November 22, 2021.

Wuthnow, Joel, *China's Other Army: The People's Armed Police in an Era of Reform*, National Defense University Press, April 16, 2019.

Wuthnow, Joel, Derek Grossman, Philip C. Saunders, Andrew Scobell, and Andrew N. D. Yang, *Crossing the Strait: China's Military Prepares for War with Taiwan*, National Defense University Press, 2022.

Xi Jinping, "A Holistic View of National Security," *Qiushi*, December 4, 2020.

"Xi Signs Order to Confer Honorary Title on Xinjiang Anti-Terrorist Squadron," Xinhua, July 5, 2021.

Xie, John, "China Is Increasing Taiwan Airspace Incursions," *Voice of America*, January 6, 2021.

"Xiplomacy: Xi's Call for China-U.S. Cooperation on Global Issues," Xinhua, November 18, 2021.

Yamazaki, Makiko, David Kirton, and Ryan Woo, "U.K. Asks Japan for Huawei Alternatives in 5G Networks: Nikkei," Reuters, July 18, 2020.

Yew Lun Tian, "China Authorises Coast Guard to Fire on Foreign Vessels If Needed," Reuters, January 22, 2021.

Yeo, Mike, and Robert Burns, "Pentagon Warns of China's Progress Toward Nuclear Triad," *Military Times*, November 4, 2021.

Yinhong Shi, "Painful Lessons, Reversing Practices, and Ongoing Limitations: China Facing North Korea Since 2003," in Carla P. Freeman, ed., *China and North Korea*, Palgrave McMillan, 2015.

Yu Jin, ed., *The Science of Second Artillery Operations* [第二炮兵战役学], People's Liberation Army Press, trans. by Gregory Kulacki, September 19, 2014.

Zhang Jiadong [张家栋], "Multi-Border War: The Possible Form of Future War" [多边疆战争：未来战争的可能形态], *Frontiers* [人民论坛·学术前沿], 2021.

Zhang Junshe [张军社], "'Three Armies and Four Seas' Drills: Deterring Those Who Conspire Against Us" [三军四海大演习：威慑图谋不轨之国], *People's Daily* [人民日报], July 29, 2014.

Zhang Xiaoming, "Deng Xiaoping and China's Decision to Go to War with Vietnam," *Journal of Cold War Studies*, Vol. 12, No. 3, Summer 2010.